LIGHT THEIR FIRE
for
GOD

LIGHT THEIR FIRE

for GOD

7

Powerful Virtues for Your Kids

ANNE AND DAVID HARPER

MOODY PRESS
CHICAGO

All Scripture quotations, unless otherwise indicated, are taken from the *New American Standard Bible®*, © Copyright The Lockman Foundation 1960, 1962, 1963, 1968, 1971, 1972, 1973, 1975, 1977, 1995. Used by permission.

Scripture quotations marked NIV are taken from the *Holy Bible, New International Version®*. NIV®. Copyright © 1973, 1978, 1984 by International Bible Society. Used by permission of Zondervan Publishing House. All rights reserved.

Library of Congress Cataloging-in-Publication Data

Harper, David (J. David), 1953-
  Light their fire for God / David and Anne Harper.
    p. cm.
  ISBN 0-8024-4292-7
    1. Christian children--Religious life. 2. Christian children--Conduct of life. 3. Virtues.
  4. Parenting--Religious aspects--Christianity. 5. Harper, David (J. David), 1953--
  Family. 6. Harper family--Anecdotes. I. Harper, Anne (Anne W.), 1953- II. Title.

BV4571.3 .H37 2001
248.8'45--dc21

00-068378

1 3 5 7 9 10 8 6 4 2

Printed in the United States of America

to our parents,
Rev. John and Sara Adkerson and
John and Sally Harper,
whose encouragement and spiritual training laid the foundation
for our knowing God

And to our children, David, Daniel, and Lauren,
whose precious lives made this book possible

Contents

Acknowledgments

When God called us to write this book, He reassured us that at the proper time He would raise up the perfect publishing company. And He did! Moody Press has truly been an instrument in God's hands as they have helped to bless millions of readers.

We'd like to thank Jim Bell, acquisitions manager, for his sensitivity to God's leading and for the opportunity to publish what God has placed on our hearts. We'd also like to thank Dave Dewitt, editorial director, for his encouragement as he oversaw our somewhat intimidating journey of editing. Our special thanks to our editor, Jim Vincent, whose patience, thoroughness, and helpful insights brought us safely to this point. We praise God for the skill He has given these men in the development and publishing of this book.

To all of our family and friends who encouraged us to write this book and supported us with prayers, phone calls, and cards, we thank you. We also appreciate Sean Lyden for helping to inspire the title and for acting as our initial editing coach. Since God often works through many counselors, we wanted to acknowledge those who helped us with proofreading, stories, tips, and Scriptures: Joyce and Keith Broome, Sue and Brad Buky, Cheryl and Dan Callahan, Kim and Wendell Couch, Teri Fite, Kay Hall, Sharon Johnson, Mal and Wanda McSwain, Lynne and Bill Warren, Regina Williams, and, of course, our parents and children.

Most of all, we make our boast in the Lord, who never calls us to do anything that He will not help us finish!

Introduction

Getting Ready to Light a Fire

When Anne first suggested we write a book together, I resisted. My reaction was, "Who would want to read it?" We do not have the usual credentials of those writing books—no advanced degrees in psychology or doctors of divinity. We are not famous, nor are our children famous. But Anne had a vision and calling for this book that only strengthened over the years. From time to time this calling was validated by family and friends who suggested that we write a book such as this.

It eventually became clear to us that this was precisely why the Lord was leading us to write this book. Although we aren't professionals, God had granted us scriptural insights and principles while we were on the firing line of growing up with our children. We received a godly heritage from our parents and grandparents who instilled in us a passion to know God and a passion to make Him known. That plus tremendous scriptural and practical training from pastors, teachers, mentors, as well as personal insights from hundreds of hours of studying God's Word, have helped us to shape the principles found in *Light Their Fire for God.*

We have seen these principles "fleshed out" in our own children as well as in other children, teens, and adults that we have taught and counseled in the past twenty-five years. Many of these topics have been presented at church, community and school seminars, and many attendees in turn are teaching these principles to others.

This is not just a book on parenting. These principles can be applied to parents and grandparents alike. Furthermore, you won't find a simple recipe for raising great kids; what you will find are time-tested principles based on God's Word that have become real to us as we have struggled through the process of raising our family.

Our three children, David, Daniel, and Lauren (now ages twenty-two, twenty, and eighteen), will soon be out of our nest entirely. We have seen Jesus come alive in their lives in a powerful way as they are seeking to follow Him. Most of our stories and illustrations are about them, so we want to express our appreciation to them for allowing us to tell some of their stories. On our last family vacation together, we read through most of the book aloud to make sure our recollections were accurate. They were thoroughly involved in the process and excited about helping us complete this project.

As Anne and I share practical, everyday experiences that illustrate the power of trusting Jesus and applying His Word, you will learn much about the Harper parents and children. You will learn of our weaknesses as well as our strengths; most of the time our greatest insights from the Lord came out of hard and even painful struggles. We hope these stories offer a fresh perspective for the everyday battlefield where we think many of today's families live.

Our material collected over the years comes mainly from Anne's note taking, from our private devotions, our talks over coffee in the morning, or driving in the car somewhere. Anne has also done most of the writing, partly due to the fact that many of the stories are hers and partly because the passion for getting the message out burns so brightly in her. Early on, the Lord led Anne to simplify her lifestyle for what we now call "the ministry of availability." She has been very intentional in backing off from most of her individual pursuits to simply be available to me and the children, either to meet me for lunch on the spur of the moment or to just "hang out" with one or all of the children.

Even as we wrote the book, God revealed new insights into what could be described as "God's Curriculum for Spiritual Development." This curriculum is for the lives of parents and their children. Theologians call the seven virtues listed in 2 Peter 1:5–7 the communicable attributes of God. Just like in the case of a communicable disease, you catch it and manifest the symptoms by spending time with someone who has the disease. We catch God's attributes and manifest His symptoms by spending time with Him. Others catch these symptoms by spending time with us. How do parents teach this curriculum of the seven virtues and help their children catch the symptoms? We believe parents can most help their children grow in the seven virtues as they both develop and model these communicable attributes of God in their own lives.

As you seek to develop these virtues in your children's lives (and in your own), remember change does not happen overnight. Progress is often being made that is barely perceptible to us as parents. I remember seven years ago having lunch with our lifelong friend and mentor, Mal McSwain, sharing with him how worried I was that David, our older son who was a ninth grader at the time, was not being the spiritual leader that I had envisioned he would be. He said, "David, remember this: the fruit does fall very far from the tree." Mal was right. I am so thankful for the leadership qualities that have become apparent not only in David, but in Daniel and Lauren as well. Often God's work in our children is imperceptible to us as parents, and many times it seems that children are wandering off the path. As parents, we simply must stay at our battle stations and trust in God's timing and His providence.

To help you apply the principles to your lives and the lives of your children, each chapter concludes with "Fan the Flame," a set of study questions. You may use this for individual study or even more effectively for discussion with your spouse or a group of other parents. "Fan the Flame" also includes "The Big Question," a key question of interpretation or application, several family activities to apply the concept to your children, and a memory verse to help your children remember an underlying truth about God and their relationship with Him. (If you are participating in a group study, start into the questions early in the week so that certain activities can be implemented prior to the group discussion. That way everyone benefits from the results that members experience.)

The book concludes with several resources for grandparents and parents, including selected verses and biblical examples that will enhance your personal time with your children. Be sure to examine them carefully; they are full of the "hidden wealth of secret places" (Isaiah 45:3). Indeed, whether you are a parent, grandparent, teacher, or coach, you can become God's instrument for helping kids find purpose and meaning in life by your practicing and sharing these seven virtues.

Our prayer for parents is that this book will inspire you to enjoy your children; they are gifts from God. You are not just raising *your* children, you are raising *God's* children, and one day they may grow up to lead you. Seek God's advice, stay in His Word, and obey His voice, and He will parent through you.

1

Strike the Match
of Encouragement

But encourage one another day after day,
as long as it is still called "Today," so that none
of you will be hardened by the deceitfulness of sin.

—HEBREWS 3:13

Years ago, before we had children of our own, I (Anne) faced a foreboding challenge that would forever shape my views on parenting. I was in my second year of teaching home economics in a local high school, grades eight through twelve. I delighted in teaching upperclassmen a myriad of skills; however, the eighth grade presented a different challenge. Those students were all forced to spend the year rotating among the related arts subjects for eight-week periods.

I had been warned by many of the teachers that I was about to encounter "the worst boy in the school." Johnny's reputation preceded him wherever he went. He was notorious for being rambunctious, disrespectful, disruptive, and totally out of control. The time came for the eighth grade classes to rotate subjects, and I determined to disregard any preconceived ideas and face Johnny with positive intentions.

As the class settled into its new routine, Johnny proved worthy of his reputation. He soon displayed his normal behavior: walking around on top of the tables, pulling students' chairs out from under them, yelling obnoxious comments, and disrupting the class at any given moment. After a few days of trying to be patient, realizing that he was obviously starved for attention, I told him in a very composed, articulate voice that I wanted to talk with him outside in the hall.

I was sure that Johnny was accustomed to being escorted from the classroom, but I suspect what came next surprised him. I had decided to use what most people call "reverse psychology"; I call it "proclaiming the truth in advance." As Johnny and I stood in the hall alone, I looked him in the eyes and said, "Johnny, I just wanted you to know how glad I am that you are in my class. People look up to you, and you have the potential of being a great leader. I think you have many wonderful qualities. We are going to have a great time in here, and I am happy to have you in my class. All right, you can go back in now."

At the risk of sounding melodramatic, Johnny went back into that classroom a different boy. Without further correction, he stopped climbing on the furniture, yelling for attention, and disrupting other students. Furthermore, he would frequently come to my desk and ask, "Mrs. Harper, is there anything I can do to help you?" I could hardly believe the transformation, but I never questioned it.

Once again, the eighth grade rotated classes, and I found myself with a new bunch of students. They were still in their first week of class, when suddenly there was a knock on my door. I was a bit startled as I opened it to see the principal standing there, and beside him was "little Johnny." In a very compelling voice, the principal said, "Mrs. Harper, Johnny does not like art, and he wants to come back to your class. Will you take him back?"

"Of course!" I said. And Johnny and I spent the last weeks of school together.

At the same time that I was teaching home economics, David was teaching English and coaching track and football at another high school. He applied the same principle of affirmation and encouragement to his students and athletes. If one of the athletes said, "I can't run the 440 yard dash!" David would challenge the runner to restate his difficult situation in another manner.

"The 440 yard dash is difficult, but as I am working to improve my speed and endurance, I can see myself doing well in this event," the student would respond. David saw tremendous transformations occur with several of the student athletes.

In football, Coach Harper and the players camped out one night on the practice field. It was just before the last day of "two-a-day" practices, and David recalls the scene:

"During that night, we sat around a lantern in a big circle. This was not planned, but we began to envision what it would be like to play for a state championship. The prior year had been a solid season, 8–2, but nothing outstanding. Our practice field was right outside the stadium, and we looked up at the stands, rehearsing what the atmosphere of the crowds would be like.

Several of the leaders began to talk about the glory days of the high school team back when they were in elementary school. "Wouldn't it be great," they said, "to see those stands filled with fans watching us win a state championship." They began to believe in themselves and their teammates.

Something very powerful happened at that moment; the team caught a vision, and that vision took root. We had no idea at that time where the state championship might be played; that decision had not been made yet. But guess what happened? That very year, in that very stadium, we played for the state championship title and won!

A LIFETIME OF AFFIRMATION

Profess the truth in advance, and you will find that it was not a lie after all. Choose a blessing rather than a curse, and a blessing will be given to you (Proverbs 11:25). If an eighth grade boy can make that kind of effort to improve his behavior, if high school football players can learn to believe in each other, think of how your *own* children could benefit from a lifetime of affirmation.

When we choose to love and encourage children when they do not deserve it, we give them hope and a glimpse of God's divine power, grace, and love—a love we did not deserve either when He took our place on the cross. Love is the greatest gift known to man, and it is the culmination of the seven virtues you are about to encounter.

Sometimes all it takes is one person loving a child with a Christ-like love to change the course of that child's life. Consider for a moment Saul in the Bible. The Lord looked at Saul's passionate influence and determination to persecute the Christians, and instead saw a man with a passion for God who would become the greatest missionary this world has ever known. It was the love with which Jesus loved Saul (Paul) that so revolutionized his life and the world.

Jesus' final desire in His "high priestly prayer" in John 17 was that we would know God so that the love with which God loved Jesus might be in us. Sounds easy—know God; love like God. But think about it; we all want to be loved perfectly, but we often find ourselves unwilling to love perfectly. Scripture gives us seven steps that we can teach our children so that they can truly know what it means to love like God loves.

Perfect love, however, is not easily acquired or taught; therefore, before we dive into the seven virtues, we must lay the foundation of praise and encouragement. It is our firm belief that with this foundation, your parenting skills will rise to a new level, and your effectiveness in teaching the seven virtues will prove successful. Within this chapter and the next, you will find many helpful tools to help you encourage your children.

THE PRAISE AND ENCOURAGEMENT GAME

One night years ago as our family gathered for devotions, an idea for a new game came to mind. We decided to all sit on the floor in a circle and "spotlight" each person as we took turns describing all of the positive character qualities we saw in that family member. We started with our youngest, Lauren, and each of us shared all of the "good things" we saw in her. Then we moved on to Daniel, David (III), Mom, and finally Dad.

The only rule was that no one could say anything negative. David was seven years old, Daniel was five, and Lauren was three. As each person came in the spotlight, Anne recorded the others' comments into one-word character qualities and saved them in a scrapbook. As of this writing, our children are now twenty-two, twenty, and eighteen. Remarkably, but not surprisingly, the lists compiled for our children (and ourselves) have hardly changed over the years. As a matter of fact, many of those attributes have been "contagious," positively affecting the rest of the family. To give you an idea of the character qualities we are referring to, below is the original list.

David	Daniel	Lauren
artistic	obedient	loving
tenderhearted	courageous	beautiful
wise	outgoing	gentle
precise	positive	persevering
honest	helpful	diligent
intense	enthusiastic	joyful
influential	determined	caring
repentant	forgiving	calm
orderly	transparent	grateful
conscientious	loyal	helpful
dedicated	humorous	thoughtful

Give yourself a moment to reflect upon the fascinating truth that God made each of us with unique character qualities that reveal part of His nature. Being able to recognize and affirm qualities in other people that differ from ours helps us to better understand the fullness of Christ's character and appreciate our differences.

Now take one of those qualities, such as "intense" or "determined," and imagine how a family could easily label that child as "bad," "rebellious," "selfish," or "mean." The repercussions of using such words, however, can be devastating on a young child now and in later years. Our prisons are full of adults who were told as children, "You are so bad," "I wish you had never been born," "You will never amount to anything," or "You idiot! You can't do anything right."

Therefore, begin to view the annoying character qualities you see in your children as future strengths—diamonds in the rough that simply need a little polishing. Let's face it; children can appear very unattractive at times in their personality, looks, and behavior. Your conscious effort to affirm your children and love them unconditionally will polish many of the rough edges; God will do the rest!

You will notice that we include two words in our game: "praise" and "encouragement." Merriam Webster's Collegiate Dictionary defines praise as "commendation; an expression of approval" for doing things well; while encouragement is an "expression that gives courage, inspires hope, or lifts the spirit."

With children and youth, we feel that it is important to stimulate doing things well and having successful actions through praise; but at the same time, through encouragement we communicate unconditional acceptance and support regardless of a child's performance. Praise focuses on positive actions, whereas encouragement focuses on character qualities. There are times when a child's performance will not merit praise, but you can always encourage a child by assigning him a positive character quality that you visualize in him. That's why in our child's life we should always light the encouragement match.

THE POWER OF PRAISE AND ENCOURAGEMENT

As we consider the power of praise, one instance stands out in our minds. When our older son, David, was in the tenth grade, the class had only one black student. Joseph (not his real name) had decided not to go on the fall class retreat, feeling that he would not fit in and was not welcomed. Many of the students finally convinced Joseph that he would surely be missed if he did not attend. Feeling somewhat accepted, he decided to join them.

One night during the retreat, a small group of students gathered around the bonfire and began to affirm one another. That may seem unusual, but this was a Christian high school, and several students recognized that showing appreciation honored God and was biblical. Gradually, more and more students joined them until the whole class stood warming their bodies by the fire and their hearts by their praise. Hours went by as one by one the students expressed their love and gratitude to other classmates.

It was during that time that many of the students expressed how much they loved, appreciated, and admired Joseph. We are sure that no one quite realized the impact of their words that night, but remarkable results followed. Solomon compared appropriate, affirming words to "apples of gold in settings of silver" (Proverbs 25:11). Those "golden words" spoken by his peers so penetrated the recesses of Joseph's heart that he returned home with a great deal more confidence. A few months later, he decided to run for class president, *and he won!*

As parents, our praise can encourage the hearts of our children. Praise leads to courage and confidence, and the Scripture commands us to "encourage one another day after day, as long as it is still called 'Today'" (Hebrews 3:13). The essence of this book has been drawn from the fact that encouragement has the profound ability to soften a person's heart. In Hebrews 3:13, the writer wrote of one believer giving courage to another; but such encouraging can also be passed from a parent to a child. In fact, *encouragement is the parent's greatest tool for preparing their children's hearts to receive the love and instruction of the Lord.*

ENCOURAGING WORDS

Some years ago, after presenting this principle to a group, a friend came to us and said, "I grew up in a family where nothing kind was said, so I don't know how to affirm my children. Would you make me a list of some things I could say to them?" The sad fact is that many families lack recognizable affirmation.

Therefore, we compiled for our friends a list of encouraging words. Maybe you too would admit, "I don't know what to say." We believe the list can help you in giving welcome words of encouragement. The list "Encouraging Words and Sentences" follows on the next page.

As a parent, you *must* study the Word of God for inspiration. Pray daily for wisdom, understanding, and discernment, and God will meet your need for giving encouragement. He will help you impart "apples of gold" at the precise moment that your child needs to hear them.

Encouraging Words and Sentences

- "You are so much fun to be with."
- "Your mommy/daddy loves you." Shorten this to "Mamma loves" or "Daddy loves" as they age. Your children need to hear those words when they are young, and when they are older it becomes cute and endearing and makes them smile. They still need it.
- "How did you learn to play so well?" (regardless of how it sounds).
- After a little job say, "Wow! You can do anything with God's help. You are so smart!" (see Philippians 4:13). Find something that they do better than you and really affirm them in that task.
- "Great job! I am so proud of you!" Explain exactly what you liked; remember that you are not looking for perfection, so leave off what he could have done better.
- "How did you get to be so smart (or pretty, handsome, or talented)?" Teach them at a young age to answer back, "Jesus made me that way."
- "I like the way you have been making up your bed (putting away your clothes, brushing your teeth, etc.)." You may even write little notes and place them on their made-up bed, dresser, or at the sink.
- "You are always so obedient!" (Proclaim the truth in advance.)
- "Thank you for being so sweet; you are always so polite and appreciative"; "I am glad that you treat others the way you would want to be treated." Affirm in advance qualities of kindness and love.
- "I noticed how nice you were to your friend today." *Catch* them doing *good deeds!*
- "You are going to be so blessed because you are reading your Bible."
- "How did you build such a great _____ (fill in the blank)? Would you teach me how to build one?"
- "I know that you will be very careful when you cross the street; you always look both ways."
- To your daughter: "You are the most precious little doll in the

world. I'm so glad that God gave you to me to take care of for Him. You are a gift from heaven." To your son: "You are a special guy. I'm glad God gave you to me to take care of for Him. You are a gift from heaven."

- "I will be praying for you today" or "I prayed for you today." Imagine telling your teenager that you will be praying for him as he leaves for a date.
- "I miss you already." (Say this before they leave to go somewhere.)
- "I've been missing you; can we spend some time together tomorrow? What would you like to do?" Then try your best to do it.
- "I really admire your (pick one): courage • positive attitude • discipline • compassion • thoughtfulness • honesty • leadership ability • grateful spirit."
- "I love you so much I can hardly stand it! But we love Jesus the most."
- "Thank you for coming home on time." Affirm when they have been obedient instead of always reacting to disobedience.

TWENTY-FIVE OTHER WAYS TO ENCOURAGE YOUR CHILDREN

Below you will find twenty-five additional ideas for encouraging your children. They are just that, ideas. There are many other ways you can inspire courage and uplift your children. Use your creativity.

1. Quote Bible verses to them such as, "The Lord bless you, and keep you; the Lord make His face shine on you, and be gracious to you; the Lord lift up His countenance on you, and give you peace" (Numbers 6:24–26). (I often quote this passage as they leave the house for school.) Another good verse is, "Be strong and courageous! Do not tremble or be dismayed, for the Lord your God is with you wherever you go" (Joshua 1:9).
2. Sing songs. Singing always lifts their spirits.

3. Pray with them. Try not to use formal prayers; simply speak from your heart.

4. Take time to play games with them and listen to them as they talk. Our children have much to teach us.

5. Bake cookies. Let them help even if they do make a mess. Then brag on how wonderful the cookies are, regardless of how they taste. When Lauren was three years old, I asked her to help me bake cookies for a ladies group. I told her many times how I enjoyed her help as she sat on the counter for a "bird's eye view." Just as we finished, she said, "Make sure you tell the ladies that it's much more fun to bake cookies with someone else."

6. Go as often as you can on their school field trips. These were special times with our children. Sometimes they would beg us to go. They were so proud to have us there and even wanted to sit with us on the bus. Enjoy those moments while they last. Take pictures of their friends with them—and be sure to make copies to give away later.

7. Volunteer to be a guest speaker for your child's class. It is also fun to show up in time to eat lunch with your child; then walk back with him or her and read the class a story. This could even be a surprise showing! David and I both enjoyed doing this.

8. Surprise your child with a birthday cake on his or her birthday to be shared with the whole class.

9. Write little notes and leave them on their pillows along with some candy when you must go out of town—even for older teens. Tell them how proud you are of them and that you know they will be fine. You might even mention how good it feels to be able to trust such wonderful children while you are gone. And be sure to write little notes, to place on occasions in their school lunches. What a pleasant surprise for him or her to uncover at lunchtime.

10. Try to expose your children to a variety of activities. You will never know where their talents lie if they are not able to try. Remember that God will use your children's talents for His glory. Be supportive of their sports, plays, band concerts, school projects, etc. Help them to be the best they can be.

Do not try to push them into something you did or did not have a chance to do. Hence, the sports enthusiast father must learn to appreciate and encourage his son's interest in playing the trumpet.

11. Fun Friday! Children love celebrating the end of a hard week at school; reward them with a special treat when they come home. (Here's one idea: rice/marshmallow treats cut into the shape of their first initial.)

12. Share with them special promises and blessings that the Lord reveals to you about them. For instance, my husband, David, was out running one day when God revealed to him that our older son had a special gift of godly discipline in his life that God was going to use for His glory. David's words inspired our son at a time when he felt that he was not particularly good at anything.

13. Volunteer to chaperone a church retreat or camp. Go and have fun. The more fun you have with them, the more they will want to have you around. Also volunteer to chaperone at other church or school activities, such as roller- or ice skating. Then skate with them if asked. At some point, you probably will be.

14. Enjoy your car rides with your children. This can be the best time to talk since you have a captive audience. Bring up interesting things that happened in your day. Ask them questions about their day. Show that you are interested. Memorize Scripture. Try not to condemn as they tell you what is on their hearts and minds. For instance, if your teenage daughter tells you that she thinks her hair looks terrible, do not say, "You shouldn't feel that way." She is more likely to continue sharing her thoughts with you if you will talk with her about some alternative hairstyles that might enhance her beauty. Most of the time they need a listening ear. Sometimes they need silence. Learn to be sensitive.

15. Lie down with them at night. When they are relaxing upon their beds, matters of the day will come flooding back. More than likely, you will hear more than your tired body can appreciate. If you will dim the lights, they will open up even

more. Never judge what they share with you, or they will stop sharing; just listen and respond with words like, "Really?" "I understand how you could feel that way"; "That must have hurt your feelings"; "What do you think you should do about it?" Help them work out solutions through Scripture and prayer. Sing songs to your children and teens to help them fall asleep. Scratch their backs. Massage their tired shoulders —then ask your spouse to massage yours.

16. Use affirming words about your children in front of them, their siblings, and your friends. They will pick up on the comments eventually. Avoid labeling a child with words such as, "She's shy," or "He's rough." Instead, choose encouraging words such as, "She has a gentle, sweet spirit," and "He has a lot of energy today." Also, try to avoid words like "You always. . ." and "You never. . ." Those statements are simply not true. Your words are very important, so choose them carefully. They *are* listening.

17. Have patience with your children. If they do not understand something you or someone else has said, do not belittle or allow anyone else (family member, etc.) to make fun of their question. Simply say, "Let me explain it again; I probably didn't explain it well enough." That goes for adults as well.

18. Try to set a goal to spend at least fifteen minutes with each child a day, even if it is spent coloring. Sometimes it takes spending a little more time with the middle child to make him or her feel equal to the oldest or youngest. But make *each* child feel special.

19. Teach your children, as they grow, to love one another and never be jealous. Do your part by never comparing your children or asking one, "Why aren't you like your older brother. If there's a baby brother or sister and you sense an older child is jealous, affirm that child in front of the baby. For instance, as you hold your baby, you might say, "You have the best big brother; you are going to have such fun playing with him when you get a little older. He is so smart and so much fun to be with." One good way to avoid jealousy among siblings is to train your children to compliment one another. Many

times I privately suggest to one child that he encourage his brother or sister. For example, I might say, "David, you need to brag on Daniel; that would really encourage him, and he would really appreciate it coming from you."

20. When a birthday arrives, take the whole family to a special restaurant to celebrate the child's special day, or fix his very favorite meal. Even if he is having a party with friends, plan a family event as well. Your child will feel very honored. This is also a great time for everyone to affirm the birthday child with praise and encouragement. You might remind them of the verse, "Those who honor Me I will honor" (1 Samuel 2:30).

21. Fathers, try establishing time for a "daddy date" with your daughters. Mothers might consider taking their sons to breakfast before school. It is a great time to have one-on-one time.

22. As you eat dinner together, ask your children to go around and tell something about their day (for example, the funniest thing that happened or their favorite part of the day). Listen when they speak. Your children will feel greatly valued if they know that you are really listening and are interested in what they have to say. Also, as you listen to each child, be sure their brothers and sisters are listening as well.

23. If your child wants to have a pet, allow him or her to have some type, even if it is a goldfish. Learning to care for something is a valuable lesson in responsibility, not to mention the fact that pets often fill a void when the child feels alone.

24. Give your child an allowance and encourage him to tithe the first 10 percent and save 10 percent before spending any. Then praise him for doing so. You may even choose a needy child to sponsor overseas, whom your child could help support. Your child will feel encouraged to know that he is helping someone in need.

25. Probably the greatest way that you can encourage your children is for you as parents to love each other—hugging, kissing, solving marital differences in a nonthreatening manner —and going on a date once a week.

IT'S WORTH THE TIME

Remember that building praiseworthy qualities in your children takes time; it rarely happens overnight. The main idea is to build an atmosphere of praise and encouragement, and this occurs when both the husband and the wife work together to create this environment. It takes years of investing your life into theirs and showing them that you are genuinely interested in their welfare before you begin to realize the dividends. Children know if you sincerely want to be with them or if you are simply "going through the motions."

Put the newspaper down, turn the television off, hang up the phone, put the golf club down, exit your computer program, and give your children some undivided attention. It does not have to be long; even ten minutes of genuine interest in their day can fill their empty tanks. If you do not, they will grow to resent the things that you love and value the most—even if what you value the most is *God*.

Undoubtedly, all parents make mistakes in parenting, but we have found that love covers a multitude of parenting errors. About seven years ago, we took our children to dinner at the top of Atlanta's Peachtree Plaza, a reward for a great year of school and good grades. While feasting on a bucket of boiled shrimp, we began to tell them how blessed we were to have such wonderful children. We were in the midst of raving about how proud we were of them and their godly character, when our middle son, Daniel, interrupted and said, "Yeah, I'm worried that [when I'm a parent] my children are not going to turn out as good as we have."

"I have been thinking about that too," interjected our older son, David. "How can we make sure that our children turn out right?"

We smiled and said, "Don't worry; they will have wonderful parents to learn from."

We could hardly believe that young teens and preteens would be pondering such a thing. Our children were certainly not perfect, and we were not perfect as parents; but when a child feels loved, accepted, and affirmed, his esteem is boosted to a level that causes him to want to please you even more. There is a fragile, thin line between a child who feels like he is "turning out right" and a child who knows he is not. You are the ones who control the line, and encouragement is the key.

Years later, during his freshman year at college, David sent us a touching letter. His encouraging words to us blessed us beyond our greatest hopes. The letter suggests the important role that encouragement plays.

Dear Mom, Dad, Daniel, and Lauren,

I hope things are going well for you all back home. You are all in my prayers. I am so blessed to have such an encouraging, loving, and admirable family; to have a mom and dad who always put God first and foremost, parents who love each other and whom I desire to emulate in my future relationship with my spouse. Being here makes me realize just how precious and special you all are to me. It's always amazing to me how many people look up to you and how much God has enriched your lives and how much He has enriched my life because of you. Despite all of my problems and struggles I often face, I still feel like I am the most loved and blessed person in the world. Thanks for always making me feel so special and for being beside me through hard times. So many people don't have the privilege of being able to come to both their parents for love and encouragement. I love you all very much! I will be praying for you, and I appreciate all of your prayers for me.

Love, David

Encouragement has its rewards. Not only will your children grow to be an encouragement to you, but they also will have the ability to encourage others. Ultimately, they will be learning to express praise and gratitude to their heavenly Father regardless of their circumstances. Learning to praise the Lord will be a blessing in their lives.

If you feel that you have fallen short in the area of encouragement, ask for forgiveness from your spouse and from your children, then ask the Lord to encourage *His* children through you so that their hearts stay soft and yielded—the perfect environment for developing the seven virtues.

F a n   t h e   F l a m e

These questions will help you fan the flame of encouragement in your family. Answer these questions and apply them. If you are reading this book with your spouse, discuss your answers; if you're in a small group, discuss your answers in that setting.

1. Why should encouragement be a part of a parent's lifestyle? (See Hebrews 3:9–12 and Hebrews 10:22–25.)

    In Hebrews 10:24 The Lord instructs us to consider one another in order to stir up love + good works

2. If you were to change something about your parenting style, what would it be and why?

    I would try to be more encouraging pointing out the good + relaxing about the negative

3. Make a list of the five greatest attributes or character qualities in each of your children. What is the value of doing this?

    Caitlin
    5. thoughtful
    1. responsible
    2. dependable
    3. loving
    4. repentant

    Olivia
    5. tender hearted
    1) kind
    2) thoughtful
    3) loving
    4. artistic

4. Next, identify for each child at least one behavior problem that
   has annoyed you in the past, then attach to it a positive term,
   and decide how you will begin to encourage that positive behavior. Discuss your ideas.

Caitlin – tongue
I know your going to become An
encourager bux using encourring words
Olivia – Laziness
I know that your going to be able to keep

5. When do you think your children feel most loved by you? *A*
   Write down your answer. Now ask each of them privately what *clean*
   you do that makes them feel loved or happy. Compare your an- *house*
   swers. *When you stick up for me*

O- playing cards + games together
Special day together

C – one on one time together

The Big Question

How will encouragement help your child know God better?

Encouragement will help my children
know God better because they
will see "Gods kindness in me."

Family Activities

Read Philippians 2:1–5 with your children. Ask them to explain what
they think it means. Then ask them what kind of attitude we are

supposed to have. Ask them what it takes to be an encourager. Help them to identify some ways they can look out for other people's interests.

Play the "Encouragement Game" with your family this week. Enjoy their responses; take notes and save them in a scrapbook.

On one night, play "Celebrate Jesus." Let each family member participate, regardless of his or her age. Focus on Jesus—talk about His goodness, His forgiveness, His love, etc. Praise Him for as many things as you can. You do not need to close your eyes. Then let the youngest child (who can) voice a simple prayer of thanks.

Memory Verse

Have your children memorize Psalm 34:1.

I will bless the Lord
at all times; His praise
Shall continually be in my
mouth

2

Fan the Flame
with Positive Words

*Let no unwholesome word proceed from your mouth,
but only such a word as is good for edification
according to the need of the moment,
so that it will give grace to those who hear.*

—EPHESIANS 4:29

Surely child rearing is the exception to the above verse instructing us to "let no unwholesome word" escape from our mouths. God would not expect us to keep our composure when our toddler has chosen to scour the new end table with a rock from the yard, or when the neighbor's child continues to bite our child. He would not expect us to stay calm when our four-year-old refuses to stay in his bed after being reprimanded for the tenth time. Would He?

God chose to reveal the importance of this Scripture in responding to children when the latter situation occurred with our son Daniel. As a baby, Daniel would never let us rock him to sleep; he would stiffen up and look around the room as if to say, "You can rock until the sun comes up, but I am not about to close my eyes. Why, I could miss something!"

When Daniel was almost four, we noticed that his personality seemed brazen and impermeable. When we tried to hug him, he would not hug us back. I remember once squeezing him and saying, "I'm going to make you love me." Several times a day David and I would tell him how much we loved him and loved being with him. Slowly, we began to see a tenderness develop. Love was progressing, but obedience was at a standstill. It seemed that his favorite pastime was seeing how many times he could get out of bed after being told, "Good night." Then it happened, an unforgettable night that astounded us both.

David and I were going through the worst night ever trying to keep Daniel in his bed. Nothing seemed to work. We tried spanking, bribing, feeding, and very stern language. Finally, we determined to hide behind our closed bedroom door.

PAINTING A PICTURE OF THE POSITIVE

To our dismay, we heard Daniel on the other side of our door, obviously willing to suffer more punishment to procure his nighttime vigil. I, David, was about to explode in anger when Anne found herself saying, "Isn't Daniel the most precious boy; he is always so obedient! He always listens to us and is so smart to go to bed when we ask him to." Catching on, I began praising our obstinate son as well. We were, of course, "proclaiming the truth in advance" (using positive words to paint a picture of the potential he *could* be). We were not lying; we were simply proclaiming the truth in advance.

Just minutes after describing Daniel's potential, that wonderful sound of silence filled the hall and our room. With great anticipation, we opened the door to find Daniel gone. Tiptoeing down the hall and turning the corner, we reached his room and found that he had returned to his bed and was sleeping soundly. We went back to our room overwhelmed that a little boy, thinking that he had accidentally overheard his parents praising his obedience, would become obedient. The sweetness of that moment was unforgettable, but it was the next morning when we really saw the genuine manifestations of professing the truth in advance.

Daniel had internalized everything he heard and awoke believing that he *was* the child spoken of so positively. Overnight, his potential had met our positive words, as he literally became our spoken word. We didn't discuss with him (until years later) what happened that night, but as far as he was concerned, he was a wonderful, obedient boy.

From that day on, Daniel's number one attribute was obedience. He is now twenty, and we can hardly remember a time, since that evening, when Daniel was ever willfully disobedient! The principle of painting a picture of potentiality is a concept that can be played out positively or negatively. Unfortunately, we have often heard parents painting a picture of their child's potential using negative words, and the child lived down to those expectations. This is why it is crucial to prayerfully consider our choice of words, having them flow out of a life submitted to the Holy Spirit.

Along with obedience came love and joy. Daniel became a great hugger, like his brother and sister. Often he grabs me (Anne), pushes me into the living room (as I play "hard to get"), throws me on the sofa, and then takes great pleasure in just sitting down beside me.

Those who know Daniel as the charismatic, joyful "pleaser" that he is, can hardly believe that he was any other way. So full of life is Daniel, that looking back we understand how at the young age of four he did not want to miss out on anything; he loves life!

Sometimes what our children need more than a spanking is a little grace, but that requires our sensitivity and recognition to the "need of the moment, so that it will give grace to those who hear." We will be the first to tell you that it is not easy. Sensitivity of that nature takes a great deal of practice, and even trial and error.

In Hebrews 5:14 we read, "Solid food is for the mature, who because of practice have their senses trained to discern good and evil." We can actually train our senses by God's Word to know if our words will be used for good or for evil. The dichotomy exists: our words can set a course for good or for evil.

A NEGATIVE TONE . . . A NEGATIVE FIRE

Concerning our words, the apostle James wrote, "The tongue is a fire . . . which defiles the entire body, and sets on fire the course of our life, and is set on fire by hell. . . . With it we bless our Lord and Father, and with it we curse men, who have been made in the likeness of God; from the same mouth come both blessing and cursing. My brethren, these things ought not to be this way" (3:6, 9–10).

Have we ever considered the fact that our tongues can affect the course of our lives and our children's lives? Jesus said that the things that proceed out of the mouth come from the heart (see Matthew 15:18). Therefore, if we desire to change our words, we must first change our hearts. Begin to pray King David's call to have God reveal what's inside the heart: "Search me, O God, and know my heart; try me and know my anxious thoughts; and see if there be any hurtful way in me, and lead me in the everlasting way" (Psalm 139:23–24). Begin to pray daily that God will search your heart and reveal your attitudes.

When the words of our mouths and the meditation of our hearts are acceptable in His sight (see Psalm 19:14), then those words that we speak to our children will become valuable in the course of their lives. As we consider Paul's confession, "I have fought the good fight, I have finished the course, I have kept the faith" (2 Timothy 4:7), we understand more of the significance of helping our children stay on "the course" with our positive words.

BEHIND THE WOODPILE

How can we teach our children to discern good and evil if we have not practiced training our own senses to discern the two? Sometimes we reprimand and spank for something we see as evil when in actuality it is the natural curiosity for that age. For instance, one day while looking out my kitchen window, an unanticipated event caught my eye. There, standing behind a pile of wood, unable to hide from my view, was my neighbor's son and another neighbor's daughter proceeding to take their clothes off. Both were about seven years old and seemed to be in a big hurry.

Responding the way I would have wanted my neighbor to have responded, I quickly called the mother, letting her know what happened. I reassured her that it was normal curiosity of children that age, but that she would probably want to know what her son was in the process of doing. I was so happy that my neighbor reacted with calm discernment and discretion in talking with him rather than spanking him.

The neighbor then calmly called the girl's mother and sent the girl home, while she talked with her son about the fact that God had made boys and girls differently. Using a simple book from a Christian sex education series, she shared with him the importance of respecting one another's private areas. Of course, the boy and girl *did* know enough to hide. Sound familiar? (See Genesis 3:7–8.)

We tell these stories to illustrate that there are positive alternatives to discipline and training that yield incredible results before you have to resort to corporal punishment. If we as parents would practice fanning the flame for obedience by using "words that edify, according to the need of the moment," then we would find that occasions for punishment would be few and far between.

THE POPCORN LESSON

One day when our son David was about eight years old, he and I had an occasion to see a movie together. While driving to the theater, we began to discuss how there is a need to express ourselves in a positive manner. I shared with him some examples and then explained that many parents give their children negative instructions and then punish them for disobedience, almost as if they were programming their children to fail.

Finishing our discussion, we entered the theater and eagerly stood in line to get popcorn and drinks. In front of us stood a mother and her young son. Interestingly, the mother proceeded to order a "barrel" of popcorn and turned to hand it to her young son while saying, "Here, hold this, and don't drop it!"

While she was paying for their popcorn, we were watching her nervous son. Sure enough, before they could turn to leave he had dropped the barrel of popcorn, spilling it all over the floor. Embarrassed, the mother jerked her son away, scolding him profusely! David and I looked at each other and simultaneously said, "She programmed him!"

Just think about it. The main word ringing in that little boy's ears was probably "drop." Now, how could the mother have fanned the flame for obedience? Simply by using different words such as, "Hold it carefully" or "Hold it tightly." Then the boy would have fixed his attention on the words, "carefully" and "tightly."

When we thoughtfully use positive statements instead of negative statements with our children, we not only encourage them to do well but also create an environment in which failure is less likely to occur.

Using positive words can also mean the difference in your child obeying or not obeying. Even if you find yourself stating something in a negative manner, you can simply restate your comment and your children will still benefit from the last words they hear you say. Look at the list below, and imagine how your child would respond in each instance.

CHANGING NEGATIVE WORDS
INTO POSITIVE WORDS

NEGATIVE WORDS	*POSITIVE WORDS*
"You are going to fall and bust your head open!"	"Be very careful playing on the jungle gym. Make sure you hold on tightly."
"You are going to put each other's eyes out if you keep doing that!"	"That stick might be a little too sharp; maybe you could play with this ball."
"I'm going to skin you alive if you don't come in here!"	"Let's see if you are fast enough to come in by the time I count to five."
"You didn't do it right! Why can't you do anything right?"	"That's great, and next time you might try adding_____."
"If you don't behave, I'm going to send you to that school/church/camp!"	"Let's practice our best behavior so that the teachers will be proud of us."
"Shut up!"	"It's time to be quiet now." Try drawing their attention to something else; "Hey, look at that_____!"
"If you don't finish that job, I'm going to spank you!"	"Let's work really hard, and then we'll have a tea party!"
"You are so bad!"	"I love you, but what you did was wrong."

Our words can create a positive or negative setting. Positive words can be full of incentives for doing better. They can cause our children to thrive. On the other hand, negative words can easily wither the spirit and will of a child. Years ago I (Anne) wrote the following poem to show the impact of our words.

Choose Your Words Carefully

"I caught the ball and tagged the base!"
Exclaimed the beaming lad.
His father quickly added, "Yeah,
But your hitting record's bad."

"I cleaned my room and made my bed,"
The girl said with delight.
Her mom in searching for a fault said,
"Did you turn off your light?"

"I made *one* A," the young boy said.
"And the rest of them were Bs!"
His dad with lowered glasses said,
"Why didn't you get *three?*"

The neighbors seemed much happier,
Joyful, and content.
The same things happened at their house
And this is how it went.

"I caught the ball and tagged the base!"
Exclaimed the beaming lad.
His father quickly picked him up
And told him he was glad.

"I cleaned my room and made my bed,"
The girl said with delight.
"You're so smart!" her mom replied.
"You always do things right."

> "I made *one* A," the young boy said.
> "And the rest of them were Bs!"
> "What? That's great!" His dad replied.
> "You studied hard, I see."
>
> A few choice words is all it takes
> For a happy home, you see.
> And what a difference words can make,
> When you choose them carefully.

ONE WORD CHANGES

The choice between two kinds of words can often spell the difference between failure and success in our children. For instance, instead of using the word *you,* try using words such as *we, us,* and *let's* when correcting. The word *you* arouses resentment and puts the child on the defensive. It is a word that will cause your child to grow up having a judgmental spirit, largely because he feels he has been judged.

This particular word change has in fact helped our marriage. Instead of David saying, "Anne, *you* need to do a better job of the laundry," he instead would say, "*Let's* (let us both) really try to keep up with the laundry so that it doesn't pile up." Of course, this will take some humility on the speaker's part, especially when he or she is not fully at fault. Of course, don't use the word *we* to imply *you. We* means both of us—your partner and you. Let's face it, we all need gentle correcting.

Furthermore, using the word *and* instead of *but* can make the statement more encouraging. Dale Carnegie expressed this idea in his classic best-seller *How to Win Friends and Influence People.* First published in 1936, the principles remain true in the twenty-first century. For instance, "Billy, you are very diligent about football practice and performing well during the games, but your grades are terrible. You have got to start studying harder!" Billy may have been encouraged until he heard the word *but.* Once he hears that qualifier, he views his parents' praise as contrived and insincere. Billy would probably not feel encouraged or motivated to improve his grades.

On the other hand, the positive alternative that fans the flame for obedience is to say, "Billy, we are so proud of your diligence when you practice and play football. You are always on time, you practice hard, and the coach likes how you play, *and* if you will apply that same great perseverance to your schoolwork, you will see the same great results!"

We will not always have the presence of mind to react with words that are "good for edification"; therefore, we must be willing to accept reminders and continue to practice. Whenever we forget and say negative things about people or situations, our children will speak up and say, "Mom or Dad, you are being negative." Of course their insights will both convict us and make us happy, for our children are mastering this principle in their youth.

You and *but* are three-letter words that should be completely eliminated from our vocabulary in such situations. Here's another: *bad*. When we label a child as "bad," we leave little or no room for that child to improve. Such words leave a child defeated and crushed in spirit. More likely this child, if consistently told that he is "bad," will grow up feeling unworthy of God's love and forgiveness. Focus on the behavior rather than the person.

Words can have a deep and lasting impact on a child's heart. In his book *When Good Isn't Good Enough,* Ron Willingham recalled the summer following sixth grade, when he decided to build a rather challenging model airplane. Willingham loved making airplanes, and he spent weeks cutting, gluing, and painting the fuselage, wings, tail, and rudders. Here is his account:

> Well, I finally finished it. And it was the most incredibly beautiful piece of work that I'd ever seen. Surely no one had ever built one that looked this good. I can still remember just standing back and admiring it—having difficulty believing that I had actually done it.
>
> I remember planning the unveiling ceremony—when I'd show it to my family. I carefully planned just the right moment—for maximum impact. As I planned the unveiling, I could even hear the applause I'd get—the raves. I even visualized all my friends and neighbors swarming in to gasp at the masterpiece I'd created. So, one evening when my whole family was in the living room listening to our Zenith con-

sole radio, I made my entrance. Inside me cymbals were clanging, trumpets blaring, and kettledrums banging!

I still remember how carefully I carried the plane so that I wouldn't damage it or drop it. I entered the room, beaming with pride, displaying the incredible creation that I'd done.[1]

Ron's anticipation was great. But his father's response was not. As Ron wrote:

"My father looked at the airplane, scrunched up his face, got this real pained look, looked at my mother and said, 'Do you reckon he'll ever learn to make one right?'"

How do you think those words made Ron feel? How would you feel? Ron detailed his reaction:

I was devastated, stunned, speechless. Immediately a big knot welled up in my throat, and I reacted the way I'd been conditioned to react in my family environment—I just stood there speechless, showing no emotion whatever. And in the next few seconds I internalized that whole massive shock. It was as if someone had crammed a hand grenade down my throat, left it lodged somewhere between my throat and my stomach, and then walked away . . . then, in a few seconds it had exploded.

I remember standing there, my emotional equilibrium destroyed, and then, without saying a word, walking out of the room. I walked outside, through the backyard to the alley, where we had large trash barrels. I remember standing beside one of them and pulling the lid off. I don't remember how much time went by.

After a while I ripped one side of the wing off . . . then the other. Then piece by piece, I crumbled up the airplane and threw it into the barrel. After doing this, I eased the lid back on the barrel and walked away—as defeated as anyone could ever be defeated.

I never again attempted to make a model plane. I never even considered it! It wasn't because I didn't want to make one . . . but that experience convinced me that I couldn't do it.

And it was as if I had no hands, no mind, no coordination, no desire—no nothing.

It had nothing to do with my actual abilities. It was all due to my negative beliefs.[2]

One cannot help but consider how the son would have reacted had the father lavished him with positive affirmation instead of crushing him with words of defeat. Ron's dad was direct, but sometimes as parents we are indirect, using sarcasm to imply the opposite of what we mean. Sarcasm is one of the most detrimental habits of speech people use. Webster's definition of sarcasm explains why: "to tear . . . speak bitterly, to cut, wince, or jeer, generally ironical. 'Sarcastic' implies intent, a taunting, sneering, cutting, or caustic remark; gibe to hurt by taunting with mocking ridicule, veiled sneers."

POSITIVE MUSIC . . . POSITIVE RESULTS

In contrast, positive words can have a positive effect on our children. As young teens, our three children became very interested in Christian a cappella, rap, and other contemporary Christian music (some of which was introduced by visiting choir members who stayed in our home). The Harper kids loved it all! Then one day, while driving our children to school, I found myself listening to an unfamiliar tape that a friend had given our older son. After leaving the school, I carefully listened to the entire tape and made mental notes of each song.

It was not the satanic music that often suggests suicide, but the words did suggest depression, apathy, and the undermining of authority. Throughout the day I prayed about and planned my strategy. I have learned over the years that people rarely change their minds simply by being told that what they are doing is wrong; they must be able to "save face" and change their minds based on *new* information presented in a positive way.

With the understanding of how much our tenth grade son, David (who was playing junior varsity basketball at the time), loved weight lifting and strength conditioning, I found discernment for the new information I would share with him. Upon his return, I calmly described the negative and condescending phrases I heard on the tape. Immediately, he began his defense for the music. I explained, "You're right. It's not evil; it's just not very positive."

Soon the younger children joined their brother around the table. We must have sat there almost one hour, discussing the topic of music. I presented to them the *new* information about the effects that music had on the body. "Medical doctors," I explained, "have shown that negative lyrics and strong dissonance have negative effects on our organs. So, if the 'wrong' kind of music can affect our bodies negatively, just think of what positive music can do for us!"

I also said, "Even if the music is good, you must also consider the lifestyle of the artist. Satan has a way of masquerading his music as good music. If Satan were going to have a concert, but the music was going to be great," I asked, "would you go?" This question obviously "struck cords" with them as they nodded in understanding. Lastly, I encouraged them, "We must be careful not to quench the Holy Spirit who is at work in us. Great music ministers to the Holy Spirit and as a result builds our spirits and bodies."

The next day, I noticed that the tape we had discussed had been replaced in the car with a new one. David, as well as his siblings, was full of new determination to build an even stronger spirit and body. He came home from school with the news of how he had shared with his friends the benefits of listening to the right type of music; some of them listened, some of them did not.

Of course, we made sure that we prayed diligently for the Lord to reward him for his obedience. A few weeks into the season, David came home saying that the varsity basketball coach had moved him up to varsity because his shooting had improved dramatically. Then David added, "I think the Lord is blessing me for listening to good music."

We must begin to realize the deep impression our words have on our children. Perhaps it would be beneficial to view our children as "wet cement." God has given us a holy responsibility to prepare our children to live for Him! The impressionable childhood years will not last long. The groundwork is laid, values are made, and the imprint is left to harden.

We are not just talking about producing good, upstanding, law-abiding, animal-loving citizens; rather, with the kindness of your words and actions you may stamp the very impression of God on their lives. In Romans 2:4, Paul wrote that God's "kindness and tolerance and patience . . . [lead] you to repentance." If we are careful, God will work through us as parents, giving us these qualities that lead our children to repentance.

THE ROLE OF GRANDPARENTS

Grandparents are in a unique position to fan the flame with positive words. Generally removed from the intense daily pressures of parenting, grandparents can often fill in the gaps that parents overlook. As a parent, welcome the input of your own parents when they are with your children. Feel free to let them read this section. (However, do not *expect* your parents to do these three things for your children. Be grateful if they do, but do not expect them to do what they are uninterested in or incapable of doing.)

If you are a grandparent, take advantage of the little moments you have with your grandchildren. The three most important things you can do for your grandchildren are: (1) encourage them, (2) pray for them, and (3) teach them God's Word. Of course, be sensitive to the desires of your children and comply with their suggestions or restrictions; do not overstep your boundaries.

In Resource One, you can read of specific suggestions in each of these three areas. Keep in mind that as a grandparent, you can help to shape your grandchild's spiritual interests by your own example and words while present. In the next chapter, you'll read how one grandparent helped our little David learn about the power of prayer.

To parents and grandparents alike, we realize that families are different, and you may not have a positive parent/grandparent relationship, but you must never give up praying and working towards that end. As a parent, if you are concerned about the faith or commitment of your parents or the negative influence they might have on your children, begin to pray for their relationship with God and your relationship with them. Who knows, some day you might find that your children have shared spiritual truths with their grandparents in ways you thought were impossible. As a grandparent, you too should be concerned for your child's wisdom and stamina in rearing your grandchildren—and their children. Pray for their energy and wisdom, and pray for a desire for spiritual dimension in their children's (your grandchildren's) lives.

As a parent, be sensitive to the grandparents' time, space, and energy when they visit; you must not expect them to do *your* job.

They have already raised their children, so try not to take advantage of them. When your family visits Grandma and Grandpa, teach your children to clean up their play areas before leaving their grandparents' house. Teach them to be polite, well mannered, and somewhat quieter than they would be otherwise. Teach them to be respectful of their *things* and space.

Help your children to display their love in tangible ways. For instance, they could bring something to their grandparents when visiting them—something that is consumable, such as cookies, crackers, soup, stationery, coffee, nuts, candy. Your children could even bring something handmade. Encourage your children to make up a poem for their grandparents at Christmas or other special occasions. The poem can describe what they like to do at Grandma's house, describe a past visit, or describe a grandparent's home.

Be positive when reminding your children to do these special things, affirming to them that *you know they will be* polite and considerate to their grandparents. Grandparents should feel very encouraged, treasuring the time with their grandchildren, and your children will remember those good times forever.

Go ahead; begin practicing positive words and watch the flame begin to warm your child's heart to the things of God.

Fan the Flame

These questions will help you fan the flame with positive words. Answer these questions and apply them. If you are reading this book with your spouse or are in a small group, discuss your answers.

1. Read Proverbs 15:1–2, 18, 30. What is the difference between positive words and harsh words? Take a moment to evaluate your words.

2. What did Jesus tell the Pharisees concerning words in Matthew 12:24–37? How can this help your family?

3. What do you think is the key to speaking positive words? (See Psalm 51:10–13 and Psalm 139:23–24 for ideas.)

4. Try using positive suggestions or remarks to your children for one full day and note the results. Share what you noticed with a friend or group.

5. List and discuss words or phrases that you feel would give grace to your children. (Refer to Ephesians 4:29.)

The Big Question

How will using positive words help your child know God better?

Family Activities

Read Ephesians 4:29–32. This is worth memorizing! Ask your children to explain the meaning. (A caution: Regardless of what a child may say, never tell him that the answer is wrong. Acknowledge the effort, and suggest—or let another child suggest—a different meaning.) Ask your children what happens when they allow unwholesome words to proceed out of their mouths. Next ask them to tell three things they will do as a result of knowing this verse. If they are old enough, have them write them on an index card.

Challenge your family to speak encouraging words to someone at school or play each day this week; then share your experiences and feelings at dinner every night.

Read Colossians 4:6 to your children; then ask them to fill in the blanks with key words. "Let your _____ always be with _____, seasoned, as if it were with _____, so that you will know how you should _____ to each person." This is a good way to help them memorize Scripture.

Memory Verse

Have your children memorize Psalm 19:14.

3

Spark an Interest in Knowing God

That I may know Him.
—PHILIPPIANS 3:10

A few years ago, I (David) took Daniel fishing on the Chattahoochee River near our house. We had been fishing for a couple of hours and had caught about ten rainbow trout, when Daniel, who was fifteen years old at the time, caught a trout that was about fifteen inches long—a much more mature, heavier fish. As Daniel began to take the treble hook out of the squirming fish, one of the hooks snagged Daniel's finger. As the fish continued flopping around in the bottom of the boat, the hook sank deeper and deeper into his finger.

I was trying to hold the fish still to get the hook out of the fish while Daniel was trying to take the other hook from his finger. After taking the fish off, we tried for about ten minutes to get the hook out of Daniel's finger. Finally I said, "Daniel, we'd better head back because we will probably need to go by the doctor's office so that he can cut the hook out of your finger."

Of course, that made Daniel try that much harder to get the hook out of his finger as we began to move down the river toward the boat launch area. Daniel was in the front of the boat and I was in the back when all of a sudden Daniel said, "I don't feel so good," and looking very nauseated, he bent forward. Then in a split second before I could get to him, he leaned back in his chair, his body stiffened, and he rolled out of the boat and into the water completely unconscious.

But before Daniel was totally submerged, I dove in after him, as our boat continued downstream. The water was neck deep as I stood on my tiptoes, trying to hold Daniel out of the water. When I first raised him up, he was still unconscious; so in an effort to revive him, I yelled, "Daniel! Daniel, Daniel!" and at the same time trying to shake him into consciousness.

Suddenly, a huge gush of water spewed from Daniel's mouth and nose, and he began flailing around in the cold water, wide awake. By this time some fishermen downriver had retrieved our boat. Daniel and I climbed into the boat and headed downstream. Except for being soaking wet, it was as if nothing had happened at all. Amazingly, during the rescue process the hook, which started this emergency, caught in my blue jeans and pulled free from Daniel's finger.

Daniel was happy about not having to go to the doctor, but for the rest of the day I sat lifeless in my chair at home saying to myself, "Thank You, Lord, that we still have Daniel."

I was so thankful that I was there for Daniel, but we will not always be available for our children when they need to be rescued. However, we can teach them to practice seven virtues that will rescue them by meeting their greatest needs. In so doing, we can create in them such an interest for knowing God that they will not be satisfied with the low view that the world has of Him. These seven virtues will help your children go beyond knowing about God to having a passion for God all their own. Knowing Jesus more intimately through these virtues is what will give them life and purpose when the world tries to pull them under. The more they learn about God and His Son Jesus, the more they will learn about themselves. And the more they learn about themselves, the more they will depend upon Jesus to meet all their needs.

BEGINNING WITH FAITH

Tucked away deep inside the Scriptures we find seven virtues that will give our children victory and keep them from stumbling blindly into deep and troubled waters. The apostle Peter wrote that those who know Christ can become "partakers of the divine nature" (2 Peter 1:4). In addition, we are promised "grace and peace" and "everything pertaining to life and godliness through the true knowledge of Him" (verses 2–3). If we apply and increase in these virtues, we will never stumble. Understanding this is the key to parenting. You are about to learn what you as a parent can do to spark an interest in your children for knowing God.

The key passage that lists the seven virtues is 2 Peter 1:5–7:

Applying all diligence, in your faith supply moral excellence, *and in your moral excellence,* knowledge, *and in your knowledge,* self-control, *and in your self-control,* perseverance, *and in your perseverance,* godliness, *and in your godliness,* brotherly kindness, *and in your brotherly kindness,* love" *(emphasis added).*

One of the first things you will notice in this Scripture passage is that the process begins with *faith*. There are two questions you may have at this point. First, "What if my child is too young to understand the gospel; can he still learn these virtues?" Second, "Why does anything need to be added to faith; if my child has Jesus, isn't that enough?" Let's begin by answering the first question.

IS MY CHILD TOO YOUNG
TO UNDERSTAND?

As parents, we can influence our children before they have a personal relationship with Christ to do what they ought to do and "flesh out" these virtues. Of course, they will not be able to practice such virtues consistently before Christ comes in and they receive a new nature (see 2 Corinthians 5:17). However, developing such virtues is a good thing. It can prepare your children for seeing both God's goodness and His wisdom in calling for such qualities in our lives. Before they are Christians, they will display these good deeds to mainly please you and others. Once they begin their relationship with Christ, God changes their motivation, making them want to live to please Him.

Whether our children have come to faith in Christ or not, our goal should be to always point them to Jesus as their standard and enabler. We can teach our children about God and His standards even before they are old enough to personally acknowledge their sin and accept His forgiveness. Doing so is to offer the Law as a model; the Law is acting as a "tutor to lead [them] to Christ" (Galatians 3:24).

The law was born out of love and forgiveness. God gave the Law to demonstrate His goodness. It was very clear and precise. It also established rewards for obedience and consequences for disobedience. Parents were instructed to diligently teach the Law to their children from morning to night. God's people were totally dependent upon the Law to know what God expected and to know how to make payment for their sins. But the Law, written on stone, was only to be their tutor until the message could be written permanently on their hearts. In the same way, we as parents are only tutors that love, forgive, discipline, and diligently point to the real thing—Jesus.

The good news is most children quickly understand that God exists (see Romans 1:20); many have the ability to understand at an early age. Furthermore, they have a sense of right and wrong "in their hearts," even as the other unbelievers do (see Romans 2:14–15).

This should remove the pressure to think that we are fully responsible for sharing every aspect of salvation to our children. Our spiritual responsibility as parents, however, comes in three phases: First, we help bring to light God's external and internal attributes that He has already made evident and placed in their hearts; we act as their tutor. Second, we need a sensitivity to be able to recognize when our child is old enough to cognitively understand the fundamentals of sin and salvation, and when they are, we need to know how to help them receive salvation. Third, after salvation, our role should be to encourage them to yield in obedience to Christ and grow in their relationship with Him.

When Daniel was seven years old, we were driving back from a birthday party and I, David, felt led to start talking about salvation and what it meant to be born again spiritually. Then Daniel asked, "How does that happen?"

I said, "That happens for someone when he understands that he is a sinner, and that God is holy. Our sin separates us from God. That is why Jesus died for our sin. If we accept what Jesus did for us and surrender our lives to Him, we are born again spiritually and will live with Him forever. This happened for me when I was sixteen years old."

Daniel responded with this question: "What happens if you don't do that?"

I explained to him, "If a person rejects Christ and dies without Him, they will be separated from God in hell forever. A person accepts Christ when he prays a prayer like, 'Lord Jesus, I am a sinner. Thank You for dying for me. I ask You to come into my heart and be Lord of my life.'" We drove on for a few moments, and I said, "When we get home we can talk about this some more, and if you're ready, you can pray to receive Christ."

Daniel said, "I just did."

THE POWER OF SALVATION

Our children can acquire some wonderful qualities before they accept Christ, but after salvation they will have a whole new perspective. When I (David) was in college, I met a guy whom I thought was the nicest guy on campus. Steve was considerate, bright, sensitive, and kind. He could hardly walk across campus without engaging in conversation with someone. Well, I thought for certain that this guy was a Christian; if anyone was a Christian, he had to be one.

A couple of years later, I found out that Steve had only recently received Christ. When I saw him, I said, "Steve, I thought that you were already a Christian." And he said, "David, I know what you mean, but the difference is now I do much of the same activities as I did before with a different motivation. Everything I did before was basically selfish; I was the center of everything. Now Christ is the center, and my motivation is to live to please Him."

Such is the difference that conversion makes. Remember, as parents we can influence our children before they have a personal relationship with Christ to do what they ought to do and "flesh out" these virtues, but only through a relationship with Christ will their motives be right—to please God—and their consistent ability exist.

Once a child (young or old) receives Christ personally, the power of the Holy Spirit comes upon him to enable him to practice and increase in all seven virtues that conform him to God's image. The Scripture declares that these virtues are useful and fruitful in the true knowledge of Christ if they are in him and are increasing (2 Peter 1:8). As a parent, you will find yourself saying, as John did of his spiritual children, "I have no greater joy than this, to hear of my children walking in the truth" (3 John 4).

No longer will your children feel powerless when the world tries to hook them and pull them overboard, for they will find strength in the true knowledge of God. It is this knowledge that will offer them:

1. The power to obey what is right in God's eye (*moral excellence,* or *goodness* NIV).
2. The power to gain spiritual insight from God's Word *(knowledge).*
3. The power to control the flesh so that the Spirit reigns *(self-control).*
4. The power to rejoice through tribulation *(perseverance).*
5. The power to please Him in all things *(godliness).*
6. The power to accept and forgive *(brotherly kindness).*
7. The power to serve God and others *(love).*

However, until a child reaches the age of accountability and is able to diligently apply these virtues personally, we parents have double duty. Not only must we be careful to study and apply our knowledge of Christ in our own lives, but we must also act on His behalf in the lives of our children. What an incredible responsibility that is. As long as we are personally practicing and increasing in these virtues ourselves, there is a level of spiritual protection made available to our children.

Take a look at Jesus' prayer toward the end of His life for His disciples:

Father, . . . I have manifested Your name to the men whom
You gave Me out of the world. . . . Now they have come to
know that everything You have given Me is from You; for the
words which You gave Me I have given to them. . . . Keep
them in Your name. . . . While I was with them, I was keep-
ing them in Your name which You have given Me; and I
guarded them and not one of them perished.

JOHN 17:5–8, 11–12

Much like Jesus, we are our children's priestly tutors and guardians until they are on their own. Ideally, the best opportunity to impact our children is when they are young; however, it is never too late to become a tutor.

NEED I ADD TO MY FAITH?

The second question you may have in regard to 2 Peter 1:5–7 is, "Why does anything need to be supplied or added to our faith? Is not faith enough?" Can a person be any more saved? Will God love him more? No, but *we* can learn to know and love Him more; and the results can be life changing. Let us explain it this way.

My interest was peaked in the ninth grade when I (Anne) discovered that there was a boy named David Harper who was tall, dark, and handsome, played sports, and was actually very intelligent. He soon became my date for homecoming. The extent of our dating that year was to meet at several school events.

However, our first real date happened in the spring of our tenth grade year when *Romeo and Juliet* was setting off sparks at the theater. We still laugh about sitting in the movie and David finally getting up the nerve to put his arm around me, and I finally reached up to hold his hand just as his arm "fell asleep." He sat there in sheer agony the rest of the movie not wanting to move his arm.

David had just accepted Christ days before, and I was looking forward to spending more time with him. Still, not knowing him very well, I often lacked topics for conversation. Occasionally, I would make notes of things to talk about and hide them in my purse, then excuse myself from the table and visit the rest room for new inspiration. Before long I did not need to make any notes of things to talk about. As a matter of fact, by the time we entered college we knew enough about each other to know that we wanted to spend the rest of our lives together.

Even though we gave each other the freedom to date other people in college, we longed to be with each other. We wrote each other nearly every day, spent hours on the phone, and visited each other as often as we could. I talked about David so much that my roommates were sick of hearing about him. (I never realized I was talking about him at all.) We lived for the day that we would get married.

We married after graduation, and we were perfectly matched, even down to the fact that we both *thought* we knew it all and had no faults. However, both of us had much to learn about the other—down to the smallest idiosyncrasies. We shared our fears, hurts, concerns, dreams, passions, and desires and began to fulfill each other's needs. We persevered through various trials together, and over time, we grew to understand unconditional love and forgiveness. It was our firsthand intimacy with one another that added meaning and value to our marriage.

Now, the knowledge that David and I have of one another is immeasurable in comparison to our early years of dating. We know each other so well, for example, that when we are sitting in church, and something catches our attention, all we have to do is just look at each other and we have communicated the same thought.

Real and genuine intimacy did not come until we were married, and yet, each day brings new surprises and growth. Likewise, intimacy with God begins only after a person has put his faith in Jesus; and it deepens as you get to know Him more fully. The more one learns and practices what pleases Him, the greater the blessing.

Believing in Christ is only the beginning of experiencing true intimacy with Him. It was John who wrote: "There are also many other things which Jesus did, which if they were written in detail, I suppose that even the world itself would not contain the books that would be written" (John 21:25). There is much to know about Jesus.

Whenever a person takes the time and effort to pursue an intimate relationship with Christ, that person gains an increasing hunger to know more and more about Him. He will get excited to read His love letters, he will find himself talking about Jesus without realizing it, and he will want to spend time alone with Him. Over time, he will come to the point where he is communicating with Jesus without saying a word.

THE SEVEN COALS

In the following seven chapters, you will discover just how significant your role is as a parent. You will also learn how to bring to light God's image in your children by teaching the seven virtues. You will discover why there is an order of succession to the virtues. You also will uncover for yourself the many benefits of practicing these seven virtues, for the seven virtues are for you first, and then your children.

David and I liken these virtues to seven coals that when stacked on top of each other and fueled with encouragement and positive words have the ability to ignite a fire. Such a fire can burn passionately for a lifetime. Nonetheless, in the same way that single coals, when pushed to the side, lose their heat, any virtue when ignored can result in a lack of truly knowing Jesus.

As your children add and increase in all seven virtues, they will not only be preserving for themselves life to the fullest with the knowledge of Jesus Christ, but they will also be kept from stumbling. This is a promise according to 2 Peter 1:8, 10: "For if these qualities are yours and are increasing, they render you neither useless nor unfruitful in the true knowledge of our Lord Jesus Christ. . . . For as long as you practice these things, you will never stumble; for in this way the entrance into the eternal kingdom of our Lord and Savior Jesus Christ will be abundantly supplied to you." What greater reason is there for teaching these virtues to our children?

God will enable you to come to your child's rescue even when you feel that you can hardly hold your own head above water. "Ask, and it will be given to you; seek, and you will find; knock, and it will be opened to you" (Matthew 7:7). Never give up asking, seeking, and knocking for God to help you in parenting. It is the little victories in your life and the lives of your children that build their faith.

THE INCREDIBLE HULK

When our son David was about four years old, he discovered *The Incredible Hulk* on television. This comic book character turned TV hero was a mild-mannered, caring man who, if provoked, would instantly burst out of his clothes and become a huge, growling beast. Soon he began to imitate the Hulk—growls and all. It was all right for awhile, but then it started to concern us. Asking him not to imitate the Hulk or not allowing him to watch the show did nothing to stop him from walking up to us and suddenly changing his personality into the Hulk. This television character seemed to be controlling his personality, and we would cringe and say that it looked like he was possessed. Needless to say, we became desperately concerned.

We have always believed in the power of prayer, so we began to pray that he would stop. Anne declared a three-day fast from food as she prayed. Neither one of us told our son David (whom we called John David at the time) that we were praying for him. But, on the third morning of Anne's fast, little David walked into the kitchen where she was preparing his breakfast and said, "I've decided to stop acting like the Incredible Hulk."

Later we told him that we had prayed and that God had answered our prayers. We tell this story because it is one of hundreds of little instances that John David remembers that sparked his interest in knowing God. Through our fasting and prayer, John David's heart was touched as he came face-to-face with God and *His* incredible power. Not only was John David inspired to pray about everything, but Daniel and Lauren were influenced as well.

Your children or teens will gravitate toward your excitement for God and His ways. Teenagers especially want to know if *this Christian thing really works,* if they can trust God with their lives, and if He really has their best interest in mind. Many parents today do not even mention God around their children. They may require that their children go to church, they may tell them to say their prayers at night, and they may even say the blessing at the table. But if our children never see us praying, reading, and studying our Bibles and talking about how great God is, they may never catch on fire for God. They, in fact, will begin looking elsewhere for excitement and fulfillment. When we are truly experiencing God for ourselves, then we should be saying things like, "Guess what the Lord showed me today?" "Wow, I just had a miracle happen!"; "I was reading in the Bible today, and look at this great verse I found!"

Practicing the principles from the first two chapters will enable you to have a positive rapport in which to influence them to know God personally. Love, encouragement, and affirmation form the foundation for which you build your training. It is an exciting adventure to watch your children grow in faith day after day and year after year.

LOST AND FOUND

After a nice visit with my parents and our children's grandparents, I (Anne) began to pile the children into the car to head home. Just then my dad—"Daddy John" to his grandchildren—stopped John David. Daddy John knew that John David, then age six, had great faith in prayer, so he asked John David to pray that he would find his glasses. "John David, would you please pray tonight before you go to bed that Daddy John would find his glasses? They have been missing for three days, and I can't remember where I put them."

Being very tired, John David said, "Daddy John, we better pray right now because I am very sleepy, and I might forget when I get home . . . Dear Lord, please help Daddy John to find his glasses; he really needs them badly. In Jesus name, Amen."

The next morning John David called his grandfather to see if he had found his glasses. "Yes!" Daddy John said.

"I knew you would," John David answered.

Daddy John later explained that he had gone down to the basement to get a screwdriver to tighten the handles on some drawers. Reaching to get the screwdriver, he accidentally dropped it on the floor next to a can of paint. At first he thought that he had been rather clumsy, but when he bent down to pick it up, there were his glasses lying on top of a can of paint. Immediately he knew that John David's prayer had been answered.

It has been fifteen years, and his grandfather remembers the episode as if it had happened yesterday. Reminding our children of how God has answered prayers in the past helps to build their faith in the present.

Celebrate Jesus! Go ahead; get excited about Him, especially in front of your children. Spend time getting to know the Lord so that you have something to talk about, just as you would your tennis match, or your new purchase, or the latest news. Soon you will begin to see greater things happen. If God knows that you are going to share the truths that you have learned with your children and others, then He will reveal more of Himself to you. Your excitement for God and His ways will become contagious.

John Henry Newman, a preacher in the Church of England at Oxford University, who would join England's reformation movement, once wrote, "Help me to spread Your fragrance everywhere I go. Let me preach You without preaching, not by words but by my example—by the catching force, the sympathetic influence of what I do, the evident fullness my heart bears to You."

What is your greatest desire for your child? What do you want her to catch from you? Is it that she become a professional athlete, or a highly paid executive, or a model, or an actress? Maybe you want your child to be a straight-A student or the most popular student in his or her class. But these things pale in significance to the one thing that assures your child of everything pertaining to life and godliness—knowing God intimately!

As we study God's Word together, we must remember that life is very complex. Applications of scriptural principles do not always offer the same results. But the one thing we can count on is that God's Word can be trusted, and He will *always* be faithful to His Word.

As your children grow, you may find that you are constantly struggling with situations or genetic factors (factors that can cause a person to be born with an unstable neurological system that can manifest itself in depression or other behavioral disorders). If so, you may need to seek help from a Christian counselor or psychiatrist who may prescribe counseling (or in some cases, medication). However, do not neglect teaching these virtues even when struggling with problems. Scripture will not return empty (Isaiah 55:11); it will accomplish what it was sent to do, though it may take years and even decades to do so.

The truths of who we are and God's care for us can lift both our children and ourselves, according to psychiatrist James D. Mallory Jr. of the Atlanta Counseling Center:

> Humans carry various scars and vulnerabilities due to the universality of sin, failure and rejection due to genetic inheritance. We are each subject to the consequences of being born into a particular situation and family. We bear scars and gifts of family interactions and suffer or benefit from the long chain of genetic tendencies our parents passed on to us. Some of us have been inadequately nurtured or hurt, others of us are physically predisposed to depression, high anxiety, alcoholism, schizophrenia, having difficulty staying on task, overreacting, and the list goes on.
>
> When we understand what it means to be made in the image of God, know our basic needs and understand the challenges our history poses for us, we are better equipped to build a life that corresponds to God's intent in creating us.[1]

Ultimately, what we seek as parents is for our children to be able to go to God and His Word by themselves and gain spiritual insight in whatever circumstances they find themselves. In the beginning, children must be spoon-fed spiritual words and thoughts. As they grow older and you have sparked an interest in them for knowing God, they will acquire a strong desire to study God's Word on their own. Therefore, over time they will not be satisfied with just milk; they will hunger for solid food.

Fan the Flame

These questions will help you spark an interest among your children in knowing God. If you are reading this book with your spouse or are in a small group, discuss your answers.

1. Read 2 Peter 1:1–15. Who is the author, and to whom is he writing?

2. Underline every time you see the word *know* or *knowledge* or any form of it. What does God want us to know, and what are the results or benefits of knowing?

3. Write down the seven virtues or qualities that we are asked to add to our faith. What do you think is the reason for the order in which they are added?

4. Read Philippians 3:8–15. What does Paul say about knowing Christ?

5. What was Paul's goal, and what fresh knowledge have you gained from studying this passage?

The Big Question

Why should we add these virtues to our faith?

Family Activities

Get up in a big bed with all your children and read to them an interesting Bible story, either from the Bible or from a Bible storybook with colorful pictures. Make it interesting. Ask questions when you have finished reading; then have a closing prayer trying to include something they have learned from the story. This is a great way to send them off to bed.

Be sensitive to the spiritual condition of your children this week, and if you think they are mature enough to understand the gospel, share some of the verses under "Verses for Children to Share the Gospel" found in Resource Two. If a child expresses a desire to receive Christ personally, be willing to lead him in a simple prayer. To be sure that he is ready, have him explain his understanding of why Jesus had to die. The prayer may be as simple as, "Jesus, please forgive me of my sins. Thank You for dying in my place. Come into my heart and live in me."

Memory Verse

Have your children memorize Psalm 46:10.

4

The First Virtue: Goodness

Add to your faith goodness.
—2 PETER 1:5 (NIV)

When our son David (whom we will call J. David for clarification) was in the seventh grade, our whole family experienced what you might call "a defining moment." J. David was beginning to gain greater independence, and we were beginning to notice some negative peer pressure starting to influence him. He tended to debate and argue, and his facial expressions often communicated discontentment.

One day when we were all at home, I (David) happened to walk into the kitchen to hear J. David talking to Anne in an openly defiant manner. As the children were growing up, we had never allowed expressions of rebellion, so when I heard J. David openly defying his mother, I became angry.

Righteous indignation rose up within me, and I reacted in a way that I would not recommend to any parents. Yelling at the top of my lungs, I grabbed J. David by his shirt just below his chin and held him up and shoved him across the room. John David became so angry that he ran upstairs, jumped on his bed, and kicked a hole in his wall. It upset Daniel and Lauren so much that they both started crying.

A few minutes later, I gained my composure and went upstairs to talk with J. David about what had just taken place. I asked for forgiveness for responding so harshly, and then we talked about what he had done wrong. During our talk, I reminded him of the right way to speak to his mother, even if he did disagree. I also told him of the importance of respecting people in authority whoever they might be. As badly handled as that was, this emotional experience seemed to nail down for J. David, as well as for Daniel and Lauren, the understanding of respect.

You will never be able to help your child grow in *goodness* if you do not first have his respect. His respect for us as parents hinges upon our consistent lifestyle and follow-through. We live what we say, say what we mean, mean what we say, and our actions support our words.

GOODNESS AS DEFINED BY THE BIBLE

As shown in 2 Peter 1:5, "moral excellence"—translated "goodness" in the New International Version of the Bible—means doing what is right as God defines what is right according to His Word. *Goodness* is the first virtue we want our children to understand.

The Bible is the standard, or plumb line, by which every action can be measured. All of our discipline, training, and influence must revolve around the Word of God. Without the biblical standard, parenting (as well as everything else) loses its meaning. This is especially important in our day because the predominant thinking of our culture does not hold to the biblical standard. Parents who do not believe in the Bible as the absolute standard of what is right and wrong will have a difficult time defining goodness.

Without an absolute standard, goodness becomes a matter of personal opinion. Personal opinions, of course, are purely subjective. If there is a disagreement between parent and child, the child can simply say that their opinion is different. If all standards are subjective, then who is to say any standard is worthier than any other? The result of not respecting God's authority is that we are left with many confused and desperate parents of troubled and rebellious youth who have no direction in life.

Therefore, if our children are to develop the virtue of goodness, we must begin by teaching the concept of respecting authority— the authority of an established standard and a person enforcing the standard. Children must learn to respect God's authority—His Word—and their parents who act as God's representatives. Without respect for authority, there is no standard for goodness to build upon.

When J. David was a senior in high school, he was asked the question, "Whom do you most admire?" He wrote, "The person I most admire is my dad because he always puts the Lord first, he loves his family, and he is a hard worker." Those were comforting words to a dad who also desired the love and admiration of his son. We believe that if children can learn what it means to be under authority, accountable for their own actions, they will begin to understand and build great faith in the authority of the Lord.

J. David is now a senior in college. Often he calls home to say, "Mom, what do you think I should do about such and such?" or "Dad, I told my friend that you give great advice and that he needed to talk to you." Our children will face many choices that will impact the rest of their lives, and if they learn to respect what we say, then they will more clearly understand what it means to respect or fear God. Of course, our authority must be based upon God's Word. As His Word has proven true in our lives, it will prove true in our children's lives as well.

THE HIGHEST AUTHORITY

Take a look at how the Bible defines itself, since we seek to establish it as our standard for goodness: "All Scripture is inspired by God and profitable for teaching, for reproof, for correction, for training in righteousness; so that the man of God may be adequate, equipped for every good work" (2 Timothy 3:16–17).

You will notice the Bible's claim that *God inspires all Scripture,* and in the Greek "inspired by God" literally means "God-breathed." We can take great comfort in teaching our children that God's Word is infallible because it is completely true.

Since goodness is based upon the Word of God, as adults we can hear or read God's Word and feel as if we are being trained, corrected, and even spanked. It is God's way of training us to have moral excellence. Moreover, God intended this training to be ongoing. The more we read and study Scripture, the more equipped we become. For instance, we may know that we are to love our neighbors as ourselves, but being obedient to that command takes a daily commitment. The Word of God is our teacher. Yet, children cannot do this for themselves. Parents must teach young children God's Word, discipline them when they are rebellious or defiant, and show them what is right. Herein lies real training and our first virtue: *goodness.*

To give you a clear picture of the process of training a child in goodness, consider the following diagram, which we call, "The Circle of Goodness."

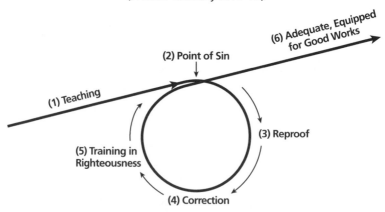

THE CIRCLE OF GOODNESS
(From 2 Timothy 3:16–17)

(1) Teaching

(2) Point of Sin

(6) Adequate, Equipped for Good Works

(3) Reproof

(4) Correction

(5) Training in Righteousness

We call it a *circle* because it repeats itself. The one thing we can count on is that there will be times of disobedience, step one; therefore, the other five steps are likewise repeated. The good news, however, is that when the circle is complete, you will have brought your child to higher ground. He will have learned a valuable lesson and you may again resume lifestyle teaching (teaching in a way that does not seem like teaching) through the way you live.

God was so good to give us a system in which to train and discipline our children. The Circle of Goodness gives us clear insight to how our children can learn goodness (moral excellence). This system will help your children begin to internalize the standard of what is right in God's sight. It will also teach your children that righteousness only comes by accepting what Jesus did in taking our punishment—by accepting Him as the Lord of their lives.

Since this type of training requires genuine love for the child (like God has for us), the primary responsibility falls to us, the parents. Teachers, coaches, relatives, and friends can help in the training process, but the ultimate responsibility resides with us. If we do not take on the job of teaching our kids, then the world will, and the world is going to teach them things that carry them away from the truth.

Let's look at the "Circle of Goodness" process described in 2 Timothy 3:16–17 to learn the steps that prepare our children for the only path that will bring happiness.

DEVELOPING GOODNESS BY *TEACHING*

Step one in developing goodness in our children is by teaching them. The word for *teaching* in the original Greek is *didaskalia,* meaning "instruction."[1] Teaching should be a positive, nonthreatening experience. With lots of training, there is little need for punishment. If we spend plenty of happy, nonthreatening time preparing and roleplaying real-life circumstances, then there is less need to discipline.

When Anne decided that it was time to potty train our oldest, she bought the book, *Potty Training in Less Than a Day.* What an exciting day it was. David ate lots of salty chips, drank plenty of water, and practiced running to the potty from every room in the house. With every victory, came great applause and yummy treats.

It was a happy, nonthreatening day, and the practice paid off in the days thereafter. Our son was trained that day despite the fact he was not physically ready until three months later. At that point, he instantly began to practice what he had already learned months prior.

Remember, prepare your child well, and good deeds will follow. And begin early; although David was not physically ready at first, the training made him want to when he was ready. The same prin-

ciple applies in the spiritual realm. Even though your child may not
be mature enough to understand the gospel, he can still be trained
so that when he is ready he can apply your teaching to his personal
relationship with Christ.

On the next page are some tips for teaching your child about right
from wrong and about consequences. All are important, but none more
so than the recommendation to "involve God and His Word in everyday situations." And so here is an important caution in using God's
Word in daily situations: *Do not sound* as though you are lecturing to
your children. Instead create a warm, open setting for learning.

One day David walked into a restaurant and observed a father and
son having breakfast. The father had a book out on the table, and he
was seriously instructing his son about spiritual matters, while the boy,
slumped over his plate, was resting his cheek in his hand. The father
was very serious, and the boy looked passive and bored. Using this type
of teaching style is not necessarily wrong if you can ask exciting and
pertinent questions based upon their interests. Learn to lighten up
and have fun.

Sharing Scripture and godly advice with our kids should be as
natural as breathing in and breathing out. If you have a passion for
God because His instructions prove true in your own life, your passionate words should rivet a child's attention. A question that we need
to continually ask ourselves is, "How much do I love God's Word?"

Whether you are a single parent or have a spouse to lead family
devotions, look forward to creative and honest discussions in a free-
flowing setting. Early in the process, I (David) mainly found out what
did *not* work. If I tried to control everybody and make them do certain things, everyone tended to resist. For example, if I asked Anne
or the children, "Did you have your quiet time today?" that tended
to promote a negative feeling as if I were a policeman checking up
on everyone.

Tips for Teaching

- Never punish children for things in which they were never trained. In reality, we deserve the punishment for not teaching them adequately. It is not enough to say, "Behave when we go to the store." We must teach them what behaving in the store is like, and what God says about being obedient to parents. It is not enough to say, "Share your toys!" We must teach them the sharing process and what God has to say about sharing in His Word. Plenty of teaching with love and affirmation will cause the child to want to be obedient.

- Work toward eliminating the need for punishment later by supplying plenty of instruction early. Make sure that your child completely understands his boundaries. Look him in the eyes, explain instructions, and ask him to repeat back to you your instructions. Let Him know what the consequences will be if he does not obey; then follow through. You will be using the same training technique that God uses.

- Choose your battles carefully. If you establish too many rules, you will be forever disciplining or "giving in." It is better to have a few rules that you can consistently keep. We have always felt strongly that the fewer the rules, the less likely the child is to break them.

- Learn to distinguish between childishness and true misbehavior. For example, spilling a cup of juice is a childish behavior; pouring juice deliberately on a friend or sibling is misbehavior. Never scold because of childishness; this sometimes requires a lot of patience. We should not expect them to be adults; they have much to learn. We should save reproof for defiance or rebellion—for sin.

- Explain your requests and even consider the child's desires. When we respond with, "Because I told you so," or "Because I'm your mother," the truth is not clearly communicated. However, if your child continues to debate your set instructions, tell him, "That's enough! End of the debate." Walk away if you must. Do not get down on his level and argue or raise your voice. You are the parent; you are the adult. Be sweet but firm.

- To see this clearly in action, read Deuteronomy 3:25–26, where God clearly told Moses He would hear no more of Moses' request to "see the fair land that is beyond the Jordan." Remember, when your children try to use persuasive words or tears or blame others, "nip it!" If this does not work, then you simply continue around the Circle of Goodness.
- Involve God and His Word in everyday situations. This will help your children to understand that everything in life (vocation, recreation, church, family, etc.) is under the lordship of Christ. Too many Christians tend to compartmentalize their spiritual life from everything else. However, when we teach our children and teens that Jesus is the hub in the wheel of our lives and that everything revolves around Him and works because of Him, they will find purpose and meaning in everything. This kind of teaching means that we need to know God's Word personally. It is a commandment, found in Deuteronomy 6:7, that we should "teach [God's Word] diligently to your sons and shall talk of them when you sit in your house and when you walk by the way and when you lie down and when you rise up."

What has worked best for us is to promote a free-flowing atmosphere. This was accomplished best when I would simply pose good questions to the family based on a practical life experience. Maybe that week I had gotten angry with someone at the office and had to ask for forgiveness. I would briefly share what happened. Then I would ask, "What is the best way to ask for forgiveness?" I'd follow up with, "Who has an example in their own life that they can share?" Occasionally, we will all pile on someone's bed. In about five minutes time, we will share prayer requests and have each family member pray for another family member. The main thing is to look for those teachable moments when you "sit" and "walk" and "lie down" and "rise up."

DEVELOPING GOODNESS
AT THE POINT OF SIN

This brings us to step two: the point of sin. The apostle James included in the definition of sin the following: "to one who knows the right thing to do, and does not do it, to him it is sin" (James 4:17). Clearly, sin is inevitable. Children will be disobedient from time to time (some more than others). We all face temptations and often sin, but how can we demonstrate to our children that sin has its consequences? Will we ignore sin and lose them to the world? Will we punish so strictly that we cut off communication with our child?

First of all, let us define sin. Simply put, sin is "missing the mark" that God has set forth in His Word. Daily we face choices that either move us toward that mark or move us farther away from the truth. And, as James pointed out, sin also is choosing not to do "the right thing." As parents, our goal should be to help our children move from sin and guilt to the point of innocence, and then onward to positive acts—those right things. In the process, we will be demonstrating the model of how we confess and repent of our sins to God and how Jesus sacrificially forgives and constantly cleanses us of guilt, bringing us back into fellowship with Him.

When sin occurs, ask yourself, "What is the best way to handle this situation?" Situations can be different, and you need to give yourself time to think before reacting emotionally or angrily. Open defiance or rebellion against your authority after the age of one (before then, they simply need plenty of love and understanding; they are building trust) should be responded to. Since God has given us this authority role as parents, we need to make sure that our parenting pleases Him. The more we are in His Word, the greater our understanding of the "mark." Step three will clarify for us the scriptural method of disciplining.

DEVELOPING GOODNESS
THROUGH REPROOF

The word *reproof* comes from the Greek word *elegcho,* meaning "to expose, convict, reprove to honor, rebuke with due measure, to censure." Solomon wrote, "Poverty and shame will come to him who neglects discipline, but he who regards reproof will be honored" (Proverbs 13:18).

One day, I (Anne) came home to find one of the garage windows broken. Soon Daniel, who was about ten years old at the time, appeared and I asked, "Daniel, what happened to this window?" His response of "I don't know" was not very convincing. I asked, "Daniel, did you break the window?" He sheepishly said, "No." Something in my spirit told me to ask again, "Daniel, did you break the window?" His next response was, "Yes."

I was happy that he had told me the truth. He went on to explain that he was locked out, and this was his way of getting in, but that he was very sorry. I decided in this case, since Daniel rarely got into trouble, that I would demonstrate for him how wrong decisions often affect people's lives. So together we measured the window. Next, we made the drive to Home Depot where we purchased the glass and other necessities to make our repair.

When we arrived home, Daniel stood and watched as I took out the molding strips, puttied the edges, replaced the glass, inserted the glazing clips, and replaced the molding. I thanked him for telling me the truth, and he never broke another pane. There are three things your children can learn as you expose sin and "rebuke with due measure." First, choosing to sin costs something. (It cost Jesus His life.) In Daniel's case, it cost him valuable playtime and money earned from his allowance. Second, our sins usually affect many more people than ourselves. Third, honesty and repentance clears our conscience and sets the matter straight.

At the point of sin, the first thing we need to do is to expose the child's wrong behavior in a way that will bring conviction. Next, we must match the level of punishment to the severity of the rebellion. When a child is punished in a just manner, he will ultimately feel *honored*. In contrast, children who grow up seldom being confronted or being disciplined inappropriately tend to feel their parents do not care for them.

Our children are going to be confronted with an evil society, and if we offer reproof when they sin, they will feel more secure and be better prepared when they leave home.

There are three common questions among parents when it comes to reproof. First, "How should we respond to our children's disobedience?" When disobedience occurs, do not respond by saying, "Why did you do that?" but rather, "What did you do?" This teaches your children *confession* of sin. If you were to say, "Why did you do that?" you are inviting your children to transfer responsibility to someone or something else and excuse themselves from any blame. Teach your children to accept responsibility for their wrong actions. If you will notice, God never said, "Why?" to Adam and Eve when they sinned.

Second, "What if our children do not accept responsibility for their actions?" Ask your child to voice what *he* did wrong without putting the blame on someone else. Teach him to say he is sorry even though he may suffer consequences. For example: "Mom, I broke the window because I was trying to get in." (Not, "Jeff was supposed to be home. If he had been, I never would have had to find another way to get in.") Then he should add, "I'm sorry; would you forgive me?" Always offer forgiveness regardless of the punishment.

Third, "What if a child is not responding well to reproof?" Make sure a love relationship exists as you apply a punishment. If the child does not feel loved, he will not accept the punishment well. Reproof to a child who already feels loved will produce conviction, and you will be able to help him make his path straight again. However, reproving your child, if the soil of his heart has not already been conditioned with love, can drive him farther away from becoming "adequate and equipped for good works." Josh McDowell, author and speaker, has often said, "Rules without relationship yields rebellion."

DEVELOPING GOODNESS
THROUGH CORRECTION

The word *correction* comes from *epanorthosis,* meaning "to correct at the time of, in connection with; to set straight again, to set upward." The goal of correction is always restoration. As Isaiah wrote, "Seek the Lord while He may be found; call upon Him while He is near. Let the wicked forsake his way and the unrighteous man his thoughts; and let him return to the Lord, and He will have compassion on him, and to our God, for He will abundantly pardon" (55:6–7).

The goal is restoration in relationship and to the path where the child is doing good deeds. The key to this concept is for the parent to *set things straight as close to the time of disobedience as possible.* There needs to be a sense of urgency in training the child to know exactly what he did wrong and exactly what he can do to make things right again. Do not allow your child to continue in disobedience; stop it at once. Reproof without correction leads to frustration. Correction gives the child the opportunity to face a positive solution to a problem. This teaches your child that when he commits his life to the Lord, he will have the ability to forsake his ways and his thoughts so that he can return to the Lord.

One thing you will notice is that there is not a fine line between steps three, four, and five. This is because each step blends into the next, making the whole process immediate and conclusive. See the next page for tips on how to correct your children.

DEVELOPING GOODNESS
THROUGH TRAINING IN RIGHTEOUSNESS

The next step in the Circle of Goodness is training in righteousness. The Greek word for *training* is *paideia,* meaning "the rearing of a child, training, discipline; sometimes involving punishment." The word for *righteousness* is *dikaios,* meaning "correct, righteous; by implication, innocent; what is right, who is right."

Training in righteousness is establishing an appropriate level of punishment and/or offering training in right behavior so that the child can feel forgiven and innocent again. This is not always easy for the parent or the child. As the Scripture notes, "All discipline for the moment seems not to be joyful, but sorrowful; yet to those who have been trained by it, afterwards it yields the peaceful fruit of righteousness. Therefore, strengthen the hands that are weak . . . so that the limb which is lame may not be put out of joint, but rather be healed" (Hebrews 12:11–13).

Tips for Correction

- Correct the child promptly. The meaning of the Greek word for *correction, epanorthosis,* helps us to understand that discipline needs to happen "at the time of" disobedience. Mothers should not "wait until Dad comes home" if at all possible. However, there are times after the mom reproves a child, when she may need to consult the father about an appropriate punishment. Parents should present a "unified front" throughout the correcting process.
- Remember that the goal is to teach the child to accept responsibility for his actions. Not learning this can lead to a multitude of problems when the child becomes an adult. When you have given a reproof by asking, "What did you do?" wait for a response until they admit what they did wrong. Then ask, "How can you set things straight? What do you need to do?" Allow them to vocalize how they will correct the problem so that they do things right in the future.
- Speak a few, well-chosen words. Much can be said with few words. Remember to choose your words carefully. A few choice words will have greater impact than many words that lose their effect and cannot be retracted! Solomon has rightly warned, "When there are many words, transgression is unavoidable, but he who restrains his lips is wise" (Proverbs 10:19).
- Make the punishment proportional to the offense. "Honor" your children by giving just treatment. Stealing from a store, for instance, deserves a greater measure of punishment than does running across the street without looking. You will find that undue punishment provokes your children to anger and will result in a loss of valuable teaching. "Fathers, do not provoke your children to anger, but bring them up in the discipline and instruction of the Lord" (Ephesians 6:4). It takes time and sensitivity to know how to match the level of punishment to the severity of the rebellion. Each situation can be very different.

There will be times when the severity of a child's behavior or their lack of willingness to repent requires a strategic level of punishment and a specific course of training to move the child to a greater level of obedience. For instance, breaking established rules—stealing, talking back to an authority figure in a disrespectful manner, acting out when told to behave, lying when told to tell the truth, pitching a temper tantrum, screaming at or hitting a parent, etc.—deserves a spanking. When the child reaches the age of about ten (this may vary according to the child and circumstance), other types of punishment should apply.

A child correctly disciplined will feel loved, secure, honored, confident, strengthened, and equipped. A great resource to have on hand is James Dobson's *Dare to Discipline*.

Look at the guidelines for properly training your children in righteousness on the next page. Spanking is an effective tool for training in righteousness, as you will see, but there are cautions to keep in mind. First, always spank in love, never out of anger; spanking in love is possible. Indeed, Scripture indicates that's how the Lord disciplines: "For those whom the Lord loves He disciplines" (Hebrews 12:6). Remember that you are "honoring" the child by bringing him to the "point of innocence." "Everyone must be quick to hear, slow to speak and slow to anger; for the anger of man does not achieve the righteousness of God" (James 1:19–20). Anger does not motivate; action does!

Second, never spank when you are frustrated with personal problems. If that is the case, try another form of discipline: time-out, quiet chair, restrictions of favorite hobbies, etc. Remember that spankings should be few and far between.

As you correct the child with appropriate discipline, try to reinforce what he has learned with applicable Scripture verses. Next, it is time to restore your child to a position of innocence. For the child to feel innocent once more, *he must ask for forgiveness, and you must forgive him!*

When, How, and What: Guidelines for Training in Righteousness

When should you use Scripture?

- Give biblical support in order to train in righteousness at the time of the offense. Make sure you do not stop with "reproof" or else you will miss out on the most important teaching. For instance, you are driving your children to school one morning, and they begin to argue and fight with one another. You feel like screaming at them and slapping their legs; however, you decide to pull off to the side of the road to reprove and correct. In your desperation to train, you say, "What are you fighting about? I'm sorry, but we are not going to school until you stop arguing" (assuming your children *want* to go to school). There is a moment of silence, and you drive off. Have you done your job in *training in righteousness?* Not until you have completed the circle. The last step is the most crucial.
- Integrate Scripture naturally, not in a preachy manner. For instance, let's return to the children fighting in the car. After exposing their behavior at the time of the incident, you ask questions, such as, "Betsy, how do you think Andy feels when you say that he is_____? Does that please God?" "Andy, are you 'repaying evil for evil'?" (Use Scripture to reinforce your words.) "What could you have said differently to Betsy?" "Betsy, how should you react next time?" This is the time to teach what is right and what to do the next time.

How can you know the appropriate level of punishment that should be used?

- Agree on the punishment beforehand with your spouse. "Prepare plans by consultation, and make war by wise guidance" (Proverbs 20:18). If you need to discuss a punishment with your spouse, do so privately, and then confront the child in complete agreement. Parents should support and defend one another. This builds respect and security in your children. Mothers should never allow the children to be disrespectful to their father, and fathers should never allow the children to be disrespectful to their mother.

- When using corporal punishment, avoid inflicting strong physical pain. Never shake an infant. Shaking is not discipline and can cause severe brain damage. Moreover, if you feel you are losing control and have left welts, bruises, or abrasions that remain after an hour or two, then you need to abandon corporal punishment as a means of disciplining your child. A recurring pattern means you may need to seek professional counseling.

- Consider other forms of punishment prior to spanking. For instance, you may try a "time-out," where they sit for five or ten minutes, rethinking their behavior. They may be required to forego dessert, a favorite television program, or even playtime with a favorite friend. Generally the thing they love the most can be withheld for punishment. Keep in mind, prior to the age of ten, spanking need not be the first form of punishment, as some children respond more readily to nonphysical discipline such as Daniel's punishment for breaking the window. And remember, after age ten or eleven a spanking can have diminishing returns, creating resentment or embarrassment to your growing child.

- Always use a neutral object when giving a spanking. Some kind of a "rod" (wooden spoon, switch, paddle, etc.) is better than using your hand when at all possible. It will help disassociate their punishment from nurturing hands.

- Make the spanking a private event. Do not embarrass the child. Tell him that he is going to get a spanking, then take him to a private room. You want to spank hard enough for it to be painful. Chuck Swindoll says that "a child's tears flush out his guilt and clear his conscience." Children desire to feel innocent. Try to be sensitive to your child's spirit; you can usually tell if they are feeling guilty over some sin; it will be written all over their face. Carrying around burdens of sin changes our demeanor.

- If your child has damaged someone else's property, make sure that he follows these same guidelines for making restitution—confession, repentance, and offering to replace or repair the

property. He should do this regardless of the attitude or unforgiveness that the offended person displays.

What should you do right after disciplining?

- Change the mood of the moment. This is the time to be ten-
  der and hug. It is the time to say, "I love you," and to affirm
  that he will do better next time. "Now let's have a happy time."
  This way the child knows your love is still there, that your action, was, in fact, an expression of your concern and care for your
  child.
- Be willing to wait if the child does not readily receive your
  words or touches of love. If the child is not ready to hug or accept your touch or words of love, he may have closed his spirit
  to you for something you said or did, or he may simply need a
  little time of reflection before he confesses. Counselor and author Gary Smalley likens a child's spirit to the sensitive tentacles
  of a beautiful sea urchin. In *The Key to Your Child's Heart* (one
  of my favorite books), he relates that when the urchin is poked
  with a stick, the creature immediately closes his tentacles and
  draws up into a hardened ball for future protection. The same
  can be true when we have offended our children, usually without knowing it. They simply close off their spirits until they
  feel safe.

It does not hurt to repeat this step if you have already forgiven
him earlier, assuming your child has quickly asked for forgiveness at
the point of sin. Teach your child how to ask for forgiveness, "I'm
sorry; I was wrong for_____; will you forgive me?" He will
need to be able to say that for the rest of his life—to God (thanking
Him for forgiving him), to a spouse, to children, and to others. Then
regardless of your emotions, *you must forgive.* You are teaching Scripture when you do this. "For if you forgive others for their transgressions, your heavenly Father will also forgive you," Jesus said. "But if
you do not forgive others, then your Father will not forgive your

transgressions" (Matthew 6:14–15). This is the most important step in the Circle of Goodness, and when you do this, then you bring your child full circle and to a higher plain. Will your child sin again? You can count on it, but the next time when he is tempted to sin in the same area that he received discipline, he will be more *adequately equipped* to respond with *good deeds.*

DEVELOPING GOODNESS:
PREPARED FOR GOOD WORKS

The last step in the Circle of Goodness is actually a destination you want to see your child reach again and again: being "adequate, equipped for every good work." The two Greek words for *adequate* and *equipped* are interesting. *Artios,* the Greek word for *adequate,* means "fitted, complete; to please, just now"; *exartizo,* the word for *equipped,* means "to complete; to equip fully; from out of."

Just as the Circle of Goodness is a process that will be repeated over and over again as new challenges face your child, the outcome of each completion is a new level of adequacy in your child. He will begin to move beyond the old challenges and become equipped for new challenges.

We should consider it a high privilege to be the ones who point the way to Jesus who is able to take our children *from out of* a pattern of destruction to the point where they are *pleasing* to God, *complete* and *fitted* for His kingdom. As parents, we end up the beneficiaries of such training as we reap the blessings of our own obedience. Third John 4 says, "I have no greater joy than this, to hear of my children walking in the truth." One day, if we do not grow weary, we will find that our children will be *complete* to serve the Lord, fixed in their position in Christ, much like that of the mature bonsai tree.

THE BONSAI TREE

The bonsai tree is a fascinating work of art. The grower of a bonsai must have great patience, time, and skill as he trains a young plant into the small image of a large tree found in nature. He takes great pains as he wires and bends the trunk and branches, training the little tree into his desired shape.

Unwanted stems are continually pruned away, the roots are periodically pruned to control the size of the tree, and water and fertilizer are added very carefully. Most people do not realize that it takes years of training the young plant before the shaped branches become fixed in their positions. The result is a fascinating miniature replica of the real thing found in nature. This type of training is precisely what God commanded us to do as parents so that our children could become miniature replicas of the real thing—Jesus!

"Train up a child in the way he should go, even when he is old he will not depart from it" (Proverbs 22:6). Just as the mature bonsai has a fixed position, so will your children when they are grown. As you diligently train your children, they will begin to fix their position in Christ. They will have the answers for some very tough questions: "Who am I?" "Why am I here?" "What is my purpose for living?" There are teenagers everywhere who do not have answers to these questions, and some, out of hopelessness, end up taking their lives. However, training based upon God's Word can help our children find a fixed position in Christ. When they go off to college or work, they will not be easily swayed, and their lives will become witnesses.

WE REAP WHAT WE SOW

During his first year of college, our son David had an opportunity to share Christ with another young man and two women after a fraternity party. They began talking about the Second Coming of Christ—of all things! One of the girls was an agnostic and engaged him in fierce debate, while his friend, Ben, listened very intently. After a while, Ben asked David how he could become a Christian. David simply led him in a prayer in front of the girls as he confessed Jesus as his Savior.

Did this conversation take place overnight? We should say not! Years of training went into that conversation. We remember many debates with a strong-willed little boy who had to learn to say things with love and respect. We remember a little boy who had to learn sensitivity and flexibility. And we remember spending many hours answering questions about God and His ways to a growing boy who only increased in his hunger for knowledge of the Bible.

The law of the harvest becomes evident as you realize that you are reaping what you sowed, later than you sowed, and more than you sowed. God will take those years of training and multiply them into a harvest of good works for Him. What a rewarding thing it is for parents to watch their children grow in their *knowledge of God and His Son Jesus* by teaching them goodness. The Circle of Goodness can be a powerful tool in your hands until your children are old enough to read and study the Bible for themselves and learn personally the importance of equipping themselves for sharing their knowledge of the Lord to others. Even then, we can still help them in applying the Scriptures to their teenage situations.

Fan the Flame

These questions will help you fan the flame in developing goodness in your children. If you are reading this book with your spouse or are in a small group, discuss your answers.

1. Read Peter's opening greeting to the churches in 1 Peter 1:1–2. Based on Peter's desire, what should be our number one reason for teaching our children the virtue of goodness?

2. Why is "being under authority" a valuable lesson for your children to learn? How can you as a parent both develop and model this in your own life?

3. In your own words explain the six steps in the Circle of Goodness (2 Timothy 3:16–17) using, if you can, a current illustration from your own family.

4. Read Psalm 14:1–3 and Romans 3:10–12. If these verses are true, what hope do we have in practicing "goodness"? (Read about two of God's names below in "Family Activities.") How can you simplify the truth of these passages in terms your child can understand? (You may want to look at some of the verses such as Romans 5:8 listed in Resource Two under "Verses for Sharing the Gospel" before writing your answer.)

5. What one principle is God teaching you about "goodness"?

The Big Question

How will practicing goodness help your child have "true knowledge" of Jesus?

Family Activities

Here are two very important names of God that you might want to introduce your children to. It is not necessary that they remember the names, but it will be valuable to know what they mean.

Jehovah Rohi means "The Lord My Shepherd." David introduces us to His name in Psalm 23—a wonderful psalm to teach your children. When your child comes to Jesus personally, he needs to know that Jesus will be his shepherd to guide, instruct, nourish, keep safe, and much more. Read to your children Psalm 23, and introduce them to their Jehovah Rohi. (Note: *Jehovah* means "Self-Existent One." Think of that; the God of the universe who needs no one desires to meet the needs of those He created in His image.)

Jehovah Tsidkenu means "The Lord Our Righteousness." We see this name in Jeremiah 31:31–34, Matthew 26:26–28, and Hebrews 8:6–13. In Jeremiah's day Judah had refused to listen to God. The people had gone their own way, and nothing except repentance and a return to righteousness (the Circle of Goodness) could save them. Jeremiah 18 is a very sad story. The people of Judah say, "It's hopeless! We are going to follow our own plans, and each of us will act according to our own (stubborn, evil) heart." God said, "My people have forgotten Me." Have you ever felt hopeless; have you ever seen it in your child's eyes? The Lord Our Righteousness is our only hope. He is the new covenant that God promised would help us know Him and remove our transgressions. Through Him we can know goodness.

Make an effort this week to ask forgiveness from your children for any wounds you may have caused them.

Finally, remember to have lots of fun with your children in the months that follow. Go camping, fishing, picnicking, or shopping. Go to the zoo or a baseball game. Plan a special activity with each child once a month or at least once a quarter.

Memory Verse

Help your children memorize Psalm 23. (Take your time helping your children learn this psalm.)

5

The Second Virtue: Knowledge

And to goodness [add] knowledge.

—2 PETER 1:5 (NIV)

Several years ago, our son David said, "Mom, I want you to remind me that I said it is not always easy to know God's will." I reminded him just the other day; he had not remembered.

The focus of this chapter will be on four "teaching" principles that will *fire up* an interest in your children in knowing God and His Word. Knowledge is the second virtue for our children, one that they add to goodness. Knowledge, *gnosis* in Greek, means "a knowing." It is a spiritual knowledge (*gnosin*) that "comes not from intellectual pursuit but . . . through the Holy Spirit and is focused on the person and Word of God."[1]

When our children apply this virtue to their faith, they can know God's will for their lives. Of course, as our son David said, knowing God's will is not always easy, but His will is not hidden from us either.

Here are four Ps for gaining knowledge of God and His will. Know these four Ps for profitable teaching, and you're on your way to increasing your children's knowledge.

PROFITABLE TEACHING:
PRESENT THE WORD

The first P of profitable teaching is *present the Word with enthusiasm*. Jesus had the incredible knack for teaching with such enthusiasm that twice people were willing to skip meals so that they would not miss a single word. Once their meal came from a boy's uneaten lunch. (Can you imagine a boy missing lunch!) Five thousand hungry people would not leave the teaching and healing of Jesus when evening was approaching, so Jesus fed them with the boy's never-ending lunch. (Read the story in Luke 9:10–17; see also John 6:9.)

Or what about the time Jesus fed four thousand who had remained with Him for three days, having had nothing to eat (Matthew 15:32)? Another time a woman who went to draw water from the well left her pot behind because she was so anxious to tell the men of the city all that Jesus had told her (John 4).

Jesus gave His disciples plenty of helpful instructions (See Matthew 10 for an example.) And when He did, it was mixed with plenty of love, compassion, and sincerity. Most of all, Jesus was a living example of what He taught.

Jesus' captivating way with words so impacted His disciples that they became willing to give up *everything* to follow Him. They knew that He had the words of eternal life. He often used examples from the Scriptures to teach them; for instance, He referred to Abraham, Noah, Job, Jonah, Isaiah, Elijah, and David. Jesus said of His own teaching, "My teaching is not Mine, but His who sent Me" (John 7:16). Knowing this, we are sure that Jesus spoke His Father's words with enthusiasm and joy. He once told His followers, "The words that I have spoken to you are spirit and are life" (John 6:63).

Later in the same passage, when many of Jesus' followers withdrew, Jesus asked, "You do not want to go away also, do you?" Peter answered, "Lord, to whom shall we go? You have the words of eternal life. We have believed and have come to know that You are the Holy One of God" (6:67–69).

A quick glance at Acts 4 reveals the disciples' enthusiastic confidence that they caught from Jesus. "Now as [the Jewish leaders] observed the confidence of Peter and John and understood that they were uneducated and untrained men, they were amazed and began to recognize them as having been with Jesus" (verse 13). When Peter and John were rebuked for speaking in the name of Jesus, they responded, "Whether it is right in the sight of God to give heed to you rather than to God, you be the judge; for we cannot stop speaking about what we have seen and heard" (verses 19-20).

By spending our time in the Word and enthusiastically teaching our children, they too will develop a passion for the Holy One of God. Significantly, the root words for *enthusiasm* are *en,* meaning "in," and *theos,* meaning "God." Thus, when we teach God's Word with enthusiasm, we are teaching *in God!* We know that it must insult God to teach His Word in a boring manner. Jim Rayburn, founder of Young Life, once said, "It's a sin to bore a kid with the gospel." Instead, we should seek to view Scripture with eagerness. King David wrote: "One generation shall praise Your works to another, and shall declare Your mighty acts. . . . They shall eagerly utter the memory of Your abundant goodness, and will shout joyfully of Your righteousness" (Psalm 145:4, 7).

One day when our son David was about three years old, he threw a deck of cards across the floor. When I told him to pick them up, he retorted, "I can't; there are too many!" Trying to respond enthusiastically with Scripture, I said, "David, yes you can! Remember, 'I can do all things through Christ who strengthens me!' Now you say that."

I stood and watched as he gathered up all the cards while repeating the Scripture verse aloud. He was so proud when he had finished.

Children will catch your enthusiasm and even try to use it on you. When Angie, my niece, was also about three years old, my sister Sharon told her emphatically that she was not to have any more Popsicles. Moments later she walked back into the kitchen and found that Angie had pushed a chair over to the freezer and was about to eat another frozen dessert. "Angela, I told you not to eat any more!" said her mother. Holding the Popsicle up in the air, Angela responded, "I can do all things through Christ who strengthens me."

Not only should we present the Word with enthusiasm, but we should also probe questions together with our children. That brings us to our second P.

PROFITABLE TEACHING:
PROBE QUESTIONS TOGETHER

Search the four Gospels for questions, and you will be astounded by how many times Jesus asked questions. Not only did He use questions to probe (to explore and investigate thoroughly) real life issues, but He also had the superb ability to respond to questions with questions of His own.

For example, look at Luke 10:25–26: "And a lawyer stood up and put Him to the test, saying, 'Teacher, what shall I do to inherit eternal life?' And He said to him, 'What is written in the Law? How does it read to you?'"

The lawyer answered by placing together Deuteronomy 6:5 and Leviticus 19:18, saying, "You shall love the Lord your God with all your heart, and with all your soul, and with all your strength, and with all your mind; and your neighbor as yourself" (Luke 10:27). Jesus said affirmed the answer, and when the lawyer followed up with the question "And who is my neighbor?" (verse 29), Jesus replied by telling the story of the Good Samaritan. Significantly, when He had finished, Jesus asked a question: "Which of these three do you think proved to be a neighbor to the man who fell into the robbers' hands?" The lawyer responded, "The one who showed mercy toward him." And Jesus said, "Go and do the same" (verses 36–37).

So probe questions with your child. Questions have a way of bringing more to an answer than just words. Questions can leave adults and children thinking about their relationship with God, their relationship with friends and enemies, their responsibility for a lost world, and their eternal destination. Questions can stir an older child's thinking about money, sex, jealousy, love, pride. You name it, questions can probe it! Ask questions, explore everyday issues, and thoroughly investigate them with your child, and you will find that your relationship will be strengthened as a result.

As parents, we should not pretend to have all the answers. A parent who comes across as "knowing everything" can be quite intimidating to a child. If you do not have an answer to your child's question, ask, "What do you think?" Even if you do know, it is a wonderful question to ask. Or you might say, "I don't know, let's look that up together." Most children love to ask questions, so probe those questions together; eventually they will go directly to God with their questions.

Our son David was always full of questions. It seemed that every time he would ask a spiritual question, we would both be so hungry to explain the answer that it usually generated more questions and stimulating discussions. Typically, younger siblings are always interested in what the oldest is doing, so of course Daniel and Lauren were all ears. Lauren said recently that because her big brother was so inquisitive about knowing the Bible, it motivated her to study more.

Keep in mind that God's greatest desire is that we acknowledge Him for the answers. One of the greatest Scriptures you can teach your children is Proverbs 3:5–6: "Trust in the Lord with all your heart and do not lean on your own understanding. In all your ways acknowledge Him, and He will make your paths straight."

The Lord God is a Father who loves to give us answers so that we might please Him. Isaiah 45:11 says, "Thus says the Lord, the Holy One of Israel, and his Maker: 'Ask Me about the things to come concerning My sons, and you shall commit to Me the work of My hands.'"

Try to answer your child's questions with Scripture; our natural hearts can be full of deceit. God's Word will personally add power and purpose to your training. Scripture promises that "the word of God is living and active and sharper than any two-edged sword, and piercing as far as the division of soul and spirit, of both joints and marrow, and able to judge the thoughts and intentions of the heart" (Hebrews 4:12).

When our hearts are full of the world, then what we teach our children will be full of error. Martin Luther once said, "I am more afraid of my own heart than I am of the pope and all his cardinals." In contrast, when our hearts are full of God's Word, then the answers we give our children have the power to "perform surgery" within their hearts. We know from our teaching experience that a word from the mind reaches a mind, but a word from the heart reaches a heart. You will enjoy probing questions together when answers from God's Word have been tucked inside your heart.

Teach your children Scriptures and Bible stories that apply to their daily situations. For instance, an insurmountable problem is an opportunity to refer to David against Goliath; being deserted by friends provides a natural opening to discuss Jesus' feelings and resources when He was deserted by His disciples. (You will find many Scripture applications for different situations in Resource Three.)

PROFITABLE TEACHING: PAINT WITH PARABLES AND WORD PICTURES

What a skillful storyteller Jesus was; He could illustrate a lesson from a word-picture like no one else. His stories included birds and lilies, sheep and goats, weddings and funerals, hidden treasures and costly pearls, salt and light, rulers and paupers, lawyers and judges, prodigals and servants. Using the agrarian setting of that day, He told stories involving sowing and reaping, vineyards and vines, roots and fruit, wheat and tares, leaven and bread, hens and chicks, specks and logs, and so much more. Some of these stories were parables, where characters and situations represented something. Others were metaphors illustrating concepts such as sacrifice and value. All taught important lessons about God, His kingdom, and those who would honor Him in this world.

With these images Jesus was teaching about everything we face today: problem solving, priorities, security, forgiveness, discipline, attitudes, purpose, peace, and love. Jesus' parables were intriguingly simple and yet the applications were profound. They left us with instructions as well as an example to follow.

Painting our teaching with stories is easy to do. Our stories need not be parables, stories created to make a point, such as the Good Samaritan of Luke 10. Instead, they can be stories based on actual experiences we have had, our children have had, or that we have read about others. Stories will leave a greater impression on our children than mere words of instruction. Even as adults, we are more apt to remember principles when accompanied with stories. Unlike instructions that usually reach only our minds, stories stir our souls (mind, will, and emotions), evoking the greatest change in our behavior.

Your stories may only be experiences from your past, but they can generate memories well into the future in your children. Here are some examples of stories we have told our children: the story of a high school friend who committed suicide, leading someone to Christ while shopping, David's coaching in the state championship game, spiteful high school peers, and a man who buried himself alive.

It is easy to use the things of nature to teach a principle. Once there were dozens of doves walking around our backyard. I called for the children and told them to watch the doves as they walked around in pairs. I explained that a male and female dove stay together for life; they are always together, and anytime you see one, you know the other one is close.

I told them about driving in my car one day when I noticed that a dove was lying in the road. Beside it stood its partner; it would not leave the other. I do not know how long it stood there, but I do know that our relationship with God is the same way. I told the children, "He is always with us and will never leave us, even in death!" Giving your child a mental picture can have lasting effects for a child, only be sure to interpret the story in godly terms. Jesus knew the value of stories and so should we.

PROFITABLE TEACHING: PRAISE THEM FOR LISTENING

The final P for profitable teaching is *praise them for listening*. When Jesus asked His disciples, "Who do you say that I am?" the following exchange occurred with Peter: "Simon Peter answered, 'You are the Christ, the Son of the living God.' And Jesus said to him, 'Blessed are you Simon Barjona, because flesh and blood did not reveal this to you, but My Father who is in heaven'" (Matthew 16:15–17). Now ask yourself, why was Jesus praising Simon Peter? Was it because Peter acknowledged who Jesus was? Or, was Jesus praising him for *listening* to the Father as He revealed truth? Peter listened and understood well.

The other day I reminded Lauren about the doves in our backyard, and before I could proceed, she said, "Mom, I remember that story." I said, "You do?" She said, "Yes, I remember everything you ever say." Wow! I had to praise her for always being such a good listener.

We should also remember that praising our children for listening often needs to *precede* teaching or instruction. One day, while her children were watching television, Melinda made a request of them. Noticing that she did not have their attention, she said, "Thank you for listening." At that all heads turned in her direction as they responded, "What did you say?" With four words Melinda had their attention! A teacher or coach can actually program his or her students to follow instructions better by thanking them for being good listeners in advance.

We need to particularly praise our children for trying to listen to God. They need to know that God works through us as parents to guide and protect them while they are young. In listening to us, they listen to God. Do not be surprised if your child comes to you and says that God is telling him something. God has spoken to many a youth—the classic example is young Samuel (1 Samuel 3:1–10)—and He can speak to your child.

Teach them to listen for what God might want to teach them. Your children will learn to listen to God from learning to listen to you. Perhaps the most important way that your children can learn to listen to God and obey His voice is by seeing it demonstrated in your own life—and telling them about His leading.

Eventually, when your child becomes a teenager, you might answer her request to go to a party by saying, "I'm not sure; why don't you go pray about it, and see what God tells you to do." You will be helping your teen to gradually transfer her submission to God. God will reward us for listening to our teens (see Isaiah 55:2–3).

Why do you think it is so important to God for us to listen? Perhaps it is because eternal life hinges upon our listening to His Word. Life in Him is truly abundant (see John 10:10); we can have as much as we desire. God's enduring Word satisfies, sustains, and strengthens us.

About ten years ago when we were teaching an adult Sunday school class, we gave the couples a set of eighty memory verse cards that Anne had typed and printed. The children still remember walking around and around a big table helping us to collate them alphabetically. When we finished, we gave each couple a set, but we were most excited about our children having them. At least we know of

three people who studied and memorized many of those verses—
J. David, Daniel, and Lauren. They still keep them by their beds.

Since they were very small, we have always rewarded them for
memorizing Scripture. We would give them fifty cents a verse. Now
they no longer need a monetary reward; they *know* the wonderful
benefits of hiding the Word in their hearts.

In Resource Two you will find valuable verses for memorizing,
handpicked for helping you and your children grow in your knowledge of God. Also in Resource Two are ideas for family devotions.
There you will find specific verses about God's Word that they can
use for family devotions.

HOW TO LISTEN TO— AND KNOW—GOD'S WORD

Over three thousand years ago, God tried to teach His people
the value of His Word by feeding them manna, bread from heaven.
Exodus 16:14–36 and Numbers 11:7–9 contain principles on "con-
suming" God's Word, the bread of heaven. Allow us to paraphrase
this passage and relate eight incredible truths that still give life to
our family. They suggest the importance of your Bible study and
presenting biblical truths to your children.

1. Gather as much as you need according to the number of persons in your family. Don't just look at it; hold it in your hands;
   gather all you need! Some days you will need more time in
   God's Word. The more children you have, the more time you
   will need to spend giving the Word. (Children and teenagers
   have different needs.) If you gather in all your family needs,
   they will have "no lack."

2. Do not leave any of it until the next day. Don't waste it or it
   will breed worms and become foul! God's Word is available
   for us every morning. If we do not eat the Word, a diseased
   world can set in. Don't waste what God is teaching you; share
   it with your family. Often, when the Lord gives Dave or me su-
   pernatural insight from studying His Word, the person thinks,
   I can't wait to tell my children what I have learned! Show your

children how to apply Scripture. As they grow older, teach them to read and study the Bible for themselves.

3. Gather it every morning while it is there. It will not keep. Read God's Word to your family every morning. Teens may have personal quiet times, but breakfast is the perfect time to feast on the bread of life together. You and your children will need it to sustain you during the day. If you miss it in the morning, you miss out!

4. Gather double portions on the sixth day and save half for the Sabbath; the Sabbath will be a day of rest. Jesus is our Sabbath, and we must prepare ourselves with the Word if we are to rest in Him! On Saturday, help prepare your family for Sunday: for worshiping together and receiving God's Word or teaching God's Word. Worshiping God on Sundays should remind us to rest in Him on a daily basis. Teach your children by example how to serve Him.

5. Bake it; boil it; grind it. Be creative in how you serve up the Word to your family. It doesn't have to be the same every day. Get excited about what you are reading or what God is teaching you, and they will catch your enthusiasm for food that satisfies. Allow them to read or share with the family. E-mail or write little verses to one another. Use the "Bread of Life" Scripture cards. Take a current event and turn it into a spiritual application. Perhaps you might spend some "red letter time." That is, looking at Jesus' words in the Gospels.

6. The manna was white. "Your word is very pure, therefore Your servant loves it" (Psalm 119:140). It is to your advantage that you teach your children that the Word of God is true and reliable. It is the one pure thing you can count on. It is the plumb line by which you measure everything else. Why is that to your advantage? Because your children will grow up trusting your advice, knowing that you rely on the pure Word of God to parent.

7. Manna was like coriander seed. "The seed is the word of God" (Luke 8:11), which is able to grow in our spirits, affecting our souls and our bodies as it grows. It only takes one little apple seed to grow an apple tree. Consider the words on the back of French's coriander spice bottle: "Coriander's warm lemon-

sage flavor and aroma add character to curries and stews and a subtle, sweet and delicate flavor to baked goods." The Word of God richly supplies *character* to our lives and *a subtle, sweet aroma* to our witness! "But thanks be to God, who . . . manifests through us the sweet aroma of the knowledge of Him in every place" (2 Corinthians 2:14; see also verses 15–16).

8. Manna tasted like wafers with honey. "How sweet are Your words to my taste! Yes, sweeter than honey to my mouth!" (Psalm 119:103). The Word of God adds sweetness to even the sourest day. Teaching our children to meditate on the Bible day and night will not only give them sweet dreams, but it will also "make [their] way prosperous and successful" (Joshua 1:8).

The manna, which God sent, was only a foreshadowing of the Living Bread who would come to earth and also teach us the importance of His Word for gaining knowledge of Him. Look at what Jesus said:

I am the bread of life; he who comes to Me will not hunger,
and he who believes in Me will never thirst. . . .
I am the bread of life. . . . I am the living bread that came
down out of heaven; if anyone eats of this bread,
he will live forever; and the bread also which I will give
for the life of the world is My flesh. . . . The words
that I have spoken to you are spirit and are life.

JOHN 6:35, 48, 51, 63

As Jesus said, quoting from Deuteronomy 8:3, "Man does not live by bread alone, but man lives by everything that proceeds out of the mouth of [God]" (see Matthew 4:4). Unless we receive this life-giving manna, we cannot live and neither can our children.

Romans 10:17 says, "Faith comes from hearing, and hearing by the word of Christ." Thus believing in the Word is our entrance to eternal life and our sustenance for the fullness of life thereafter. Just as the children of Israel were sustained by the manna in the wilderness for forty years until they reached the Promised Land, we too must become satisfied on the Word of God for our entire lives until we reach our promised land—heaven!

THE ROLE OF BIBLE STUDY IN PRAYER

Interestingly, you will find that when your children and you study and meditate upon the Word of God, often everyone will be led to pray. Praying is like the icing on the cake of the Word of God. The more we teach our children to meditate (ponder and whisper to yourself) on God's Word, the more they will desire to pray to God throughout the day. They should soon discover that Bible reading leads to accomplishing another command to "pray without ceasing." (By the way, 1 Thessalonians 5:17 is a great memory verse for your kids to learn.)

George Mueller was a man of vigorous faith who totally depended on God through His Word and through prayer to meet the needs of the orphanages he had established in England. He said,

> The first great and primary business to which I ought to attend every day was to have my soul happy in the Lord. The first thing to be concerned about was not, how much I might serve the Lord, how I might glorify the Lord; but how I might get my soul in a happy state, and how my inner man might be nourished.
>
> Before this time my habit had been to give myself to prayer after having dressed in the morning. Now I saw that the most important thing I had to do was to give myself to the reading of the Word of God and to meditation on it, that thus my heart might be comforted, encouraged, warned, reproved, instructed; and that thus, whilst meditating, my heart might be brought into (an experiential) communion with the Lord.
>
> The result I have found to be almost invariably this, that after a very few minutes my soul has been lead to confession, or to thanksgiving, or to intercession, or to supplication; so that though I did not, as it were, give myself to prayer, but to meditation, yet it turned almost immediately.[2]

Finally, remember that knowledge will include, at times, admonishment. As Paul wrote, "And concerning you, my brethren, I myself also am convinced that you yourselves are full of goodness, filled with all knowledge and able also to admonish one another" (Romans 15:14). Therefore the virtue of knowledge must be supported with lots of love, encouragement, and plenty of family fun. When so supported, this coal burns brightly.

Fan the Flame

1. *Jehovah-Mekoddishkem,* another important name for God, means "I Am the Lord Who Sanctifies You." Read John 17:15–19. How does the Lord sanctify us? Does the Holy Spirit play a part?

2. There are two meanings for "word" in John 17. In verses 14 and 17, the word is *logos,* the written (or spoken) Word of God. In verse 8, the word used is *rhema,* a specific and personal message from God as revealed by His Holy Spirit. Have you ever read a verse or heard something preached that pierced your inner most being? That was God giving you a personal message. This becomes very significant when it comes to teaching our children to listen for God to instruct them throughout the day. In the description of the spiritual armor, the apostle Paul wrote to "take . . . the sword of the Spirit, which is the word of God" (Ephesians 6:17). The word for "word" is *rhema.* What specific truths can you now share with your children about this verse?

3. Do the Scriptures cited above shed extra light on this virtue of knowledge? If so, how?

4. Isaiah 55:6–11 is one of the most riveting passages in all Scripture. How can this passage help you as a parent?

5. What steps of action will you take in helping your child to practice the virtue of knowledge?

The Big Question

How will practicing knowledge help your child have true knowledge of Jesus?

Family Activities

Read and examine 2 Timothy 3:16 and Hebrews 4:12 with your children. Be sure to mention that "inspired" means "God-breathed." This verse should be familiar to you by now.

Make sure your children have their own Bibles as soon as they can read, and choose appropriate versions for their age brackets.

Establish an award system for Scripture memory. Make a big deal over their Bible study and memory verses. Let them know that the Scriptures they learn when they are young will always be with them! You can begin with the memory verses that conclude each "Fan the Flame" section.

Use Psalm 103:17–18 as a prayer of praise and commitment to the Lord today!

Memory Verse

Have your children memorize Psalm 119:11. If they are older, consider having them memorize verses 9–11, or have them memorize Psalm 1:2.

6

The Third Virtue: Self-Control

And in your knowledge, [add] self-control.
—2 PETER 1:6

*I*t was 11:30 at night. David and the children (around the ages of two, four, and six) were sleeping peacefully. I, on the other hand, was downstairs in the kitchen frantically sweeping the floor for overnight company soon to arrive. After murmuring and grumbling for awhile about my heavy burden of child rearing, housekeeping, no help, and on and on, I stopped abruptly, put my hands on top of the broom, and burst into tears. "I'm so tired," I said. "I'm just so tired."

Then those desperate words came out of my mouth, those words that only the most unfit have dared to say: "I feel like just getting in my car and driving off and never coming back!"

Wow! I quickly thought. *Now I know how those mothers feel who actually do leave their families.*

And then God spoke through His Word: "No temptation has overtaken you but such as is common to man; and God is faithful, who will not allow you to be tempted beyond what you are able, but with the temptation will provide the way of escape also, so that you will be able to endure it" (1 Corinthians 10:13). It was like the Lord grabbed me and said, "Look, you are not alone in this temptation; I faced it too." I thought of His temptation in the Garden of Gethesemane: "If it is possible, let this cup pass from Me; yet not as I will, but as You will" (Matthew 26:39). And then He brought another verse to mind, "We are destroying speculations and every lofty thing raised up against the knowledge of God, and we are taking every thought captive to the obedience of Christ" (2 Corinthians 10:5).

As parents, you will have attacks from the enemy that will come against the "knowledge of God" in which you are trying to increase. So will your children. Moreover, the tempting thought may even seem to make sense. As Solomon warned, "There is a way which seems right to a man, but its end is the way of death" (Proverbs 14:12). There is a sharp contrast between what the world says and what the Word of God says, and yet so often we are fooled. Consider the basic differences between the words of the world—contemporary society—and the words of God—the Scriptures:

The World Says:	**The Word Says:**
Get all you can get.	It is better to give than to receive.
You deserve a break.	Do your work heartily as unto the Lord.
Be number one.	Humble yourself under God.
Spread that rumor.	Hide one another's transgressions.
You need money, prestige, and power.	Be content with godliness.

THE SOURCE OF SELF-CONTROL

The apostle Paul wrote of the source of self-control in Romans 8:5–8:

Those who are according to the flesh set their minds on the things of the flesh, but those who are according to the Spirit, the things of the Spirit. For the mind set on the flesh is death, but the mind set on the Spirit is life and peace, because the mind set on the flesh is hostile toward God;

for it does not subject itself to the law of God,
for it is not even able to do so, and those who are in the flesh
cannot please God (emphasis added).

We do not have to "muster up" self-control; it is actually a result and part of being focused on the Spirit; it is one of the fruit of the Spirit (Galatians 5:23). As we "set our mind" on the Spirit and are completely devoted to pleasing Him rather than ourselves, we find strength for adding self-control. When we "love the Lord . . . with *all* [our] heart, . . . soul, and . . . mind" (Matthew 22:37, italics added), the things of the world that tempt and taunt us seem insignificant. "The love of Christ controls us" (2 Corinthians 5:14) as we set our mind on Him.

As parents, we all have the same deeply felt concerns that our children will not listen when God speaks to them, instead listening to and being drawn into the many temptations that surround them. Paul had that concern for the new believers in Corinth. "But I am afraid that, as the serpent deceived Eve by his craftiness, your minds will be led astray from the simplicity and purity of devotion to Christ" (2 Corinthians 11:3). Even though self-control is just a matter of focusing on the Spirit rather than the flesh, there is nothing passive about it. It is a matter of being proactive and alert and passionately aggressive about defending "goodness" (doing right in the sight of God) and "knowledge" (a Holy Spirit-revealed knowledge).

IT'S A BATTLE

If overcoming temptation were going to be an easy task, Paul would not have described it in warlike terms like "destroy," "take captive," and "escape." Temptation *is* a battle—a battle between the spirit and the flesh. The diagram on the next page, "When Temptations Come," will help our children and us to understand the battle of temptation. The three circles, one inside the other, represent our whole person. The inner circle represents the spirit, where the Holy Spirit indwells believers. The second, or middle circle, represents the soul. The outer circle represents the "flesh," or body. Our body is not evil, but as an instrument weakened by sin, it is vulnerable to the world's influence, satanic forces, and our own fleshly desires. Temptation must invade and take captive our mind (the cognitive part of the soul) if it is to reach our inner spirit.

WHEN TEMPTATIONS COME

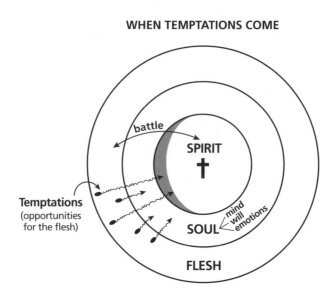

The flesh desires to serve itself, while the Spirit desires to serve God; hence, there is a battle. The flesh will always be bombarded with opportunities; we must create opportunities for the Spirit. Before we talk about strengthening our spirits, we want to point out the weakness of the flesh.

Temptation is at its peak when desire and opportunity meet. For instance, let's say that you are walking through the mall heading for the bookstore. On your way you pass an ice cream shop. *That looks good,* you say to yourself. But you don't really have the desire for ice cream at the moment, so you pass it up and reach the bookstore. On another day, you are walking through the mall toward the bookstore when all of a sudden you begin to have a desire for ice cream (not that there is anything wrong with ice cream). Your desire becomes stronger and stronger, and before reaching the bookstore, to your right you spot an ice cream shop. You think to yourself, *What an opportu-*

nity! That is just what I was craving. Nothing short of divine intervention will keep you from getting ice cream at that point.

Because temptation is at its peak when desire and opportunity meet, what we set our desires on becomes very significant. When our desires are set on the flesh, temptations are allowed to set up camp in our flesh; they move toward the Spirit for battle, securing, if they can, strongholds in the soul. The Spirit, more powerful than any temptation presented to us, can easily combat the temptation. However, if our desires are not set on pleasing the Spirit, the enemy can come at us with surprise attacks because the opportunities will always be there.

When we give in to the desires of the flesh, the Spirit becomes wounded. This is sin; Scripture tells us not to grieve the Holy Spirit. Once we realize that we have allowed the Holy Spirit to be wounded, we must quickly ask for forgiveness and be healed. Otherwise, continuous battle scars of the Spirit can cause our spirits to become callused. When calluses form around our spirit (the inner man), the Holy Spirit has difficulty influencing the soul and the flesh. For this reason, we are told in Romans 13:14 to "put on the Lord Jesus Christ, and make no provision for the flesh in regard to its lusts."

Battles are won or lost at the threshold of the mind. We either take the temptation captive by lining up our thoughts with the Word of God (our "way of escape") or allow temptation to cross the threshold and hold us captive. Giving in to the temptation is what leads to sin. "His own iniquities will capture the wicked, and he will be held with the cords of his sin" (Proverbs 5:22).

Being held captive is not unlike the situation faced by prisoners of war. The action movie *Rambo* included vivid images of emaciated American soldiers held captive by the North Vietnamese. Peering helplessly through the bamboo bars stood those weary, forlorn men with gaunt faces, rotten teeth, scraggly beards and hair, with hardly a will to live. That's the picture of captives of sin. King David described it this way: "When I kept silent about my sin, my body wasted away through my groaning all day long. For day and night Your hand was heavy upon me; my vitality was drained away as with the fever heat of summer" (Psalm 32:3–4). Paul, in all his transparency, explained the battle this way:

*I do not understand; for I am not practicing what I would like
to do, but I am doing the very thing I hate. . . . So now, no
longer am I the one doing it, but sin which dwells in me. . . .
For I joyfully concur with the law of God in the inner man,
but I see a different law in the members of my body, waging
war against the law of my mind and making me a prisoner of
the law of sin which is my members. Wretched man that I
am! Who will set me free from the body of this death?
Thanks be to God through Jesus Christ our Lord!*

ROMANS 7:15, 17, 22–25

Do you ever feel as if you are living in a war zone at home?

"YOU ARE NOT ALONE"

To hear the words, "You are not alone," is usually a great comfort. That is the truth with temptation. Is your child tempted to lie, steal, throw temper tantrums, hit or push at impulse, argue and talk back, destroy other people's property? Relax; he is not the only one. We want to share with you three universal truths about temptation that you and your child will benefit from. They are simple. They are comforting. They are the truth. *1. All temptation is common to man. 2. God is faithful with an escape. 3. Every temptation has a counteracting truth (our way of escape).*

It is interesting that the original Greek word for *self-control* is *egkrateia,* meaning *mastery.* Self-control was certainly on God's mind when He intervened in the first recorded sibling rivalry between Cain and Abel (Adam and Eve's first sons). When the brothers brought their offering to the Lord, Abel brought "the firstlings of his flock and of their fat portions." Even though not specifically mentioned in Genesis 4:4, we can infer that the two brothers were well aware of what God required. Hebrews 11:4, 6 says that, "By faith Abel offered to God a better sacrifice than Cain, through which he obtained the testimony that he was righteous . . . And without faith it is impossible to please

Him, for he who comes to God must believe that . . . He is a rewarder of those who seek Him."

So what did Cain bring? Cain "brought an offering to the Lord of the fruit of the ground." Though Cain was a tiller of the land, God had requested otherwise. The Lord's response is significant. After God showed "no regard" for Cain's sacrifice, "Cain became very angry and his countenance fell. Then the Lord said to Cain, 'Why are you angry? And why has your countenance fallen? If you do well, will not your countenance be lifted up? And if you do not do well, sin is crouching at the door; and its desire is for you, but you must master it'" (Genesis 4:5–7). God was telling Cain that he must rule, reign, and have dominion over sin. And in so doing He created a dramatic word picture: *"Sin is crouching at the door, . . . but you must master it."*

I can only imagine the sin that lay crouched behind the door had I chosen to act on the thought that had come that night, when I said "I feel like just getting in my car and driving and never coming back." But when I chose to receive and apply the Word of the Lord at the moment of my temptation, my whole countenance was lifted, in the same way God had described would happen if Cain would "do right."

Before our children can know God as *El Shaddai,* the "All-sufficient God" who instructs them in the way they should go and meets their every need, they must first know Him as *Adonai,* "Lord and Master." The name Lord indicates a relationship in which we are in total submission to His will. Take a look at what Jesus said in the Sermon on the Mount, "Not everyone who says to Me, 'Lord, Lord,' will enter the kingdom of heaven, but he who does the will of My Father who is in heaven. . . . Therefore everyone who hears these words of Mine, and acts on them, may be compared to a wise man who built his house on the rock. And the rain fell, and the floods came, and the winds blew and slammed against that house; and yet it did not fall, for it had been founded on the rock" (Matthew 7: 21, 24–25).

This Scripture passage clearly explains why we should teach our children to have self-control. The Lord will speak to them, either through us or by His Word. If they learn how to reject their own desires and act upon His Word, there is peace and protection in the Lord. With obedience comes victory. Therefore, we must help our children to exercise self-control (mastery; acting upon His Word) so that they can master the sin that will come against their practicing "knowledge" (knowing God) and "goodness" (doing right in the sight of God). Resource Three includes Scriptures you can use with your children to teach them the benefits of the Holy Spirit and how various people in the Bible either learned or failed to practice self-control—and the outcomes.

"WHERE IS MY BREAKFAST?"

When our son J. David was six years old, he walked into the bedroom where I was getting ready and put his hands on his hips and said, "Where is my breakfast? Why aren't you downstairs fixing my breakfast like you should be?" Astonished, I said, "Look, you are not going to intimidate me. I am not taking that from you. You can just go downstairs and fix your own breakfast."

Can you believe it? He was already a Christian and had already had a great deal of training in "honoring parents" and "obeying God's Word." Yet here was this little boy who sounded like an old man who had never learned any virtues at all. My husband and I began to feel sorry for his future wife; we were already envisioning marital problems if we did not intervene quickly. A quick remedy was to start buying "breakfast bars." However, the long-term solution was not as easily acquired.

In time, David began to get a grip on self-control, becoming very sensitive and understanding. The Word of God oversaw the whole process. We could only instruct and warn; David had to learn to control the temptation that caused him to disobey God. He learned to take captive those thoughts that would cause war within his spirit and with us. His strengths, which once rubbed us the wrong way, we now admire. We have watched him grow from wanting to please himself to wanting to serve others, while still maintaining his strength as a leader. The Lord is gracious, and He is the one who is faithful with the results when we are obedient to put His Word into practice.

THE WAY OF CAIN

You teach your child what is right so that things will go well for him, and you are pulling so hard for him in your thoughts and prayers that he will do right. But it is still up to him to be obedient. Cain, for instance, heard from God but did not listen. Instead, afterward, "when they were in the field, . . . Cain rose up against Abel his brother and killed him" (Genesis 4:8).

At this point you may be asking yourself, "Wait a minute. Where was God when this innocent man was being killed?" But God does not force us to do His will. He instructs and warns us, and is pulling for us to make the right choices. When we do, there is reward, but when we sin, He disciplines us.

And so it is with your child. The choice is his. If the child chooses to submit to the flesh and serve himself, he deprives himself of knowing God's will and experiencing His peace. But if by faith he chooses to submit himself to the lordship of Christ, he finds that God's grace and peace are multiplied to him. In 2 Peter 1, where the seven virtues are found, Peter began his letter by saying, "Grace and peace be multiplied to you in the knowledge of God and of Jesus our Lord" (verse 2). It is incredible to think that we would gain a greater understanding of God and Jesus our Lord (our master whom we serve, not ourselves) as we add self-control. Moreover, grace and peace are two of the benefits of obeying Him and acting upon His Word. It is a spiritual battle; therefore, we grow spiritually when we set our mind on the Spirit rather than the flesh.

DRESSED FOR COMBAT

Before a soldier leaves for combat, he goes to boot camp to learn how to be a knowledgeable, loyal, and disciplined soldier. He receives a great deal of training and practice while there. Most soldiers head to war with a passionate desire to fight for what they believe is right. They are also trained to be able to recognize the enemy and are equipped with the necessary armament and tactics to stay alive. Everyone faces the same enemy no matter where he finds himself on the battlefield. However, all the training and discipline that he receives in the safe environment of boot camp is still only head knowledge until he faces the reality of war and employs his training. He then begins to understand the meaning of sacrifice and self-control.

Imagine that the draft board called your son and told him that

he must leave tomorrow to fight in a war overseas. You would probably be saying, "That's ridiculous! What unconscionable and irre-
sponsible government would send a young, unskilled, and undisciplined
boy off to fight a war they expect to win?" Yet parents do it every
day, raising children and sending them off to school and into the world
without teaching them the disciplines needed to have victory over
the enemy.

Likewise, there is a season of parental control similar to boot camp
in which parents can help their children develop habits and spiritual
disciplines in a safe environment before they confront the enemy
alone. The spiritual goal of the parent should be to move the child
from being under parental control to having self-control. We do not
want our child to walk away from the battle, to be absent without
leave (AWOL). Yet we know that the flesh is likely to go AWOL
since it is a spiritual battle. Therefore, our child's greatest need is that
his spirit be reinforced, before and after he becomes a Christian.

If your child is not yet a Christian, he will be totally dependent
upon you to expose sin, to reveal the truth, and to explain that his
greatest enemy has already been judged (John 16:9–11). Your child
needs to know that as he obeys you (God's representative), he is obeying God, and there is reward in obeying Him. My grandmother used
to quote to us all the time when we were growing up, "No good thing
does He withhold from those who walk uprightly" (Psalm 84:11).
Your child would greatly benefit from hearing this daily.

Once the child has accepted Christ personally, you will need to
help him to know the importance of listening to the Holy Spirit.
You will be moving your child from parental-control to self-control,
and he will begin to master sin on his own because he has been taught
to recognize and obey the voice of God. Of course, His voice will not
be audible, but God will communicate truth to him through his mind
and spirit if he truly seeks Him.

Jesus said, "But when He, the Spirit of truth, comes, He will guide
you into all the truth; . . . He will glorify Me, for He will take of Mine
and will disclose it to you" (John 16:13–14). How can we help our
children build up their spirits and minds so that they will be able to
recognize God's voice?

THE WEAPONS OF OUR WARFARE

On pages 118–21 you will find fifteen tips for teaching self-control. These tips all involve using weapons of spiritual warfare. God has provided us with spiritual weapons as we help our children add self-control. As the Scripture reminds us, "For the weapons of our warfare are not of the flesh, but divinely powerful for the destruction of fortresses." (2 Corinthians 10:4).

There are three main weapons that we can use in the battle of self-control:

1. The Word of God
2. Prayer
3. Faith

These three weapons guard our spirit and inform our mind, wills and emotions—our soul—so we can resist the temptation that come against our flesh. This is shown in the diagram "Power of Our Spirit." When the Word of God, prayer, and faith reinforce the spirit, our soul and flesh are influenced. The result is that our actions prove we are Christians.

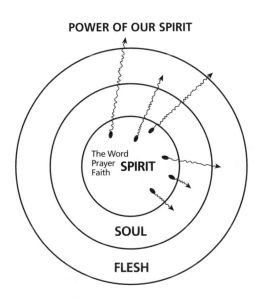

POWER OF OUR SPIRIT

The Word
Prayer **SPIRIT**
Faith

SOUL

FLESH

Tips for Teaching Self-Control

Self-control comes when we use our spiritual weapons—the Word of God, prayer, and faith, to resist temptation and those things that gratify ourselves instead of others.

1. Pray in the morning with your children about the things they will face during the day so that they stay alert to temptations that would cause them to do other than they should. For example, pray with them for their willingness to share toys when friends come over, being kind to brothers and sisters, and obeying parents.

2. Set up a system for Scripture memory and rewards that apply to their immediate and future needs. Make it fun, using charts with stars, fifty cents a verse, or whatever you believe would motivate your child. Some of our favorite verses were short but practical—and powerful: "Do all things without grumbling or disputing," "Do not let kindness and truth leave you," and "Never pay back evil for evil" (Philippians 2:14; Proverbs 3:3; Romans 12:17). My husband and I still laugh as we remember when one of our children would hit the other and then quickly say, "Never pay back evil for evil!"

3. Christian schools are great for reinforcing what you are trying to teach at home, including memory verses. David, our oldest, started attending a Christian school in the ninth grade, and Daniel and Lauren started in middle school. If your child attends a public school, he needs to be reminded constantly that he is on the mission field, and you will need to increase your prayer coverage for him. Encourage him to find some accountability partners at the school.

4. Stretch your children's faith by telling them to fall backward into your arms, or take them on a faith walk by blindfolding them and giving them directions as they walk.

5. Practice replacing temptation with truth—truth based upon God's Word. For example, if they complain, tell them to make a list of ten things for which they are grateful. If they are bored, assign them a chore. If they are unkind to a sibling, do something kind (such as making their sister's bed).

6. Let your children have a tea party to practice being polite and saying kind things to one another.

7. When grumbling or complaining arises, try singing or praising. One night our children stayed up waiting for some cousins to come spend the night. When we finally received word that it was too late and that they would come the next day, all three children began to grumble and complain. Finally, we said, "All right, everyone stop complaining; we need to thank God anyway because He may have been sparing them from an accident. We don't know what could have happened to them tonight; so let's go around and everyone praise God that the cousins are not coming over tonight." Well, it worked! When they finished, they were at peace.

8. Set boundaries. When your children are babies, you will definitely need a parent-controlled home (feeding, sleeping, etc.). Later, sometime between ages nine and eighteen months, try using a playpen to form a boundary. Start with just a few minutes and gradually increase the time, even if they scream to get out. Around two to four years of age, try having a "quiet time" when they have to sit quietly for a time and entertain themselves (making a puzzle, coloring, etc.). Boundaries will not only help your child learn to honor other people's space, but boundaries will also help your child to grow up with a greater sense of security and control over his own space.

9. Duty charts also help develop self-control. Besides memory verses, charts can be adapted for chores and goals. Try having a "Good Behavior List" where good behavior is matched with a reward. Always try to program for "good" rather than for "bad"; such as a "bad behavior list."

10. Teach them to come when you say, "Come," that "No" means no, and that they should obey quickly and cheerfully. My husband's sister, Kim, says that if her children do not obey quickly *and happily,* they are spanked; if they throw a temper tantrum for being spanked, they are spanked again. It has definitely worked! Her motto is that "It is much harder to erase bad habits than to start good ones."

11. Allow your children to pick their chores within a set allotment. For example, when our children were young, we told them that they could pick whether they wanted to vacuum, dust, or clean the bathrooms. They each picked a different one, then monthly they would rotate jobs. Have "folding up parties"; young children can be taught to fold their own clothes.

12. Even if you have all the money in the world to spend on your children, do not allow them to have everything they want; hold back. Teach them the importance of giving and serving. Not long ago, newscaster Maria Shriver shared some of her parenting methods with the media. She explained that she drives her children to school (they do not take a limousine). Her children set and clear the table and clean up, they spend time with their mother serving the needy, and they have certain responsibilities. We thought that might be of inspiration to some of you.

13. Teach your children: "Guard your downtime." Temptations are always stronger when we are not striving for a goal or vision. Therefore, help your children set goals. Assure your children of downtime by not allowing them to do everything they want to do—even if they are good things. Do not let them become overcommitted. When we asked our son, Daniel to tell us what he thought about self-control he said, "Tell them not to let their children do too much and be overcommitted." We might add, he was our child who did not want to miss out on anything, and we had to hold him back many times.

14. Make sure that your family members keep their commitments. Do what you say you are going to do. Encourage your children to follow through with their commitments. As mentioned above, help your children to limit their commitments, so they can uphold each commitment they make.

15. The best way to teach self-control to your children is to demonstrate yielding to the Spirit rather than the flesh in your own life. To serve God and one another is perhaps the key to overcoming the desire to serve the flesh. (We will discuss this more in chapter 10.) As the apostle Paul wrote, "For you were called to freedom, brethren; only do not turn your freedom

into an opportunity for the flesh, but through love serve one another" (Galatians 5:13).

As you study the "Tips for Teaching Self-Control," keep in mind you are actually teaching your children to use those three spiritual weapons that will help them overcome temptation and loss of self-control: the Bible, prayer, and faith. We strongly recommend the use of Bible memorization for overcoming temptation. (Resource Three includes a list of Bible verses suitable for memorizing that can help children resist temptation in twenty different areas.)

Federal agents employed by the U. S. Treasury spend their time studying real dollar bills so that when a counterfeit bill comes along, they can detect it instantly. The same is true spiritually. In every way, Satan is the counterfeit of Jesus Christ, which explains why we are so often fooled by things that pop into our minds. The practice by the Treasury Department agents to recognize the counterfeit is a good illustration to use with your children as you teach them to detect the "real thing" as they read, study, memorize, and apply the Bible as early as they are able.

Jesus defeated Satan in the wilderness by quoting Scripture. There is hardly time at the moment of temptation to say, "Wait a minute; I need to go and read my Bible to find a good verse to use." Therefore, our children (and we) need to learn it so that they (and we) can speak it in the way Jesus did. Psalm 119, the longest chapter in the Bible, is full of the beneficial qualities of God's Word. Help your children memorize some of them, such as, "Your word have I treasured in my heart, that I may not sin against You," and "How can a young man keep his way pure? By keeping it according to Your word" (verses 11, 9).

Not only can we use the Word of God as a weapon, but we also have prayer as a weapon. One of the most touching accounts in the Bible is found in Matthew 26:36–46, when Jesus' disciples could not stay awake long enough to pray with Him. At the time, Jesus' soul was "deeply grieved, to the point of death." When He found them sleeping after asking them to pray, Jesus said, "So, you men could not keep watch with Me for one hour? Keep watching and praying that you may not enter into temptation; the spirit is willing, but the flesh is weak" (38, 40–41). Right now we are praying that the Lord would drive that home for all of us. We simply do not pray enough!

Faith is the third weapon we can sharpen in our battle to practice and teach self-control. As simpleminded humans, we simply need the faith that obeying Jesus is going to pay off. One evening, Lauren began to take bowls out and ingredients to make banana pudding for a class at school. Since we were going to be eating dinner shortly, I asked her if she would instead empty the dishwasher and make the pudding after dinner. Very respectfully she said, "OK," and quietly switched jobs. I was once again reminded of her sweet obedience that she has always displayed, and I hugged her and told her how much I appreciated her consistent obedience.

Then Lauren said, "Sometimes I just get tired of doing everything I'm supposed to do." I could only smile and say, "I know, Lauren; sometimes I feel the same way" (not that either one of us always does things right). Then the Lord reminded me of a verse that I began quoting: "Let us not lose heart in doing good, for in due time we will reap if we do not grow weary" (Galatians 6:9). Lauren recognized the verse and quoted with me the final words.

Sometimes our faith grows weak and weary, and we doubt that it really pays off to hang in there and do what the Lord says rather than what the world is telling us to do. Jesus said, "The thief comes to steal and kill and destroy; I came that they may have life, and have it abundantly" (John 10:10). It is easy to lose faith when life seems unfair.

Paul had to remind a young Timothy to "fight the good fight of faith" (1 Timothy 6:12). We can help our children to do the same, and a key way is helping them to develop the virtue called self-control.

F a n   t h e   F l a m e

1. Satan does not want us to have self-control over what we know to be right (goodness and knowledge). How can you and your children defeat him? (Review 1 John 2:13–14.)

2. Many of the questions your children might have concerning temptation are answered in the following verses: James 1:13–17; Hebrews 2:17–18; 4:15–16. Read these verses, then think of three or more questions that these Scriptures answer. Write down the questions and the answers to have them ready for your family discussion.

3. Since battles are won or lost on the threshold of the mind, how would you explain Daniel 1:8–9 to your children? What would you like for them to learn from this passage? (You might need to do some background reading in the previous or latter verses.)

4. Examine these names of God, then tell how they can be significant in helping your child practice self-control: *Adonai* means "Lord and Master"(used in Matthew 7:21–23; Luke 6:46); and *Jehovah–nissi* means "The Lord is my Banner (of victory)" (used in Exodus 17:15; Deuteronomy 25:17–19) God's enemies must be subdued—Amalek (in Deuteronomy 25) is a picture of the flesh.

5. List the three main weapons of our warfare, and then plan an attack against the greatest battle your family is facing. (Include specific verses and written prayers.) You might find helpful verses in Resource Three.

The Big Question

How will self-control help your child know God better?

Family Activities

Your child will need a paper plate, some seeds, and some glue. The seeds can all be the same or from three different fruits or vegetables. Have them draw three concentric circles on their plate so that the plate has three divisions. Label the center circle, "spirit." Label the middle circle, "soul," and label the outer circle, "flesh."

Then, using stickers, pictures, or words, label the spirit circle with "Bible," "Prayer," and "Faith," preferably around the inner edge of the circle so that "spirit" can be seen in the middle. In the middle circle (soul) have them write the words, "Mind, Will, Emotions." (These are the three things that make up the soul.) Read Galatians 5:16–17, and explain how we need to make our spirits strong (or "hearts" if you prefer) by reading God's Word, praying, and having faith in God.

Next have them draw squiggly lines from their seeds out into the flesh area as if the seeds were growing. Teach your children that as the Word of God, prayer, and faith grow, they will help us to think good things, want to do the right things, and be joyful and thankful. Then as the seeds grow farther, they help our bodies to act the right way.

This activity can be modified to fit the ages of your children.

Memory Verse

Have your children memorize Galatians 5:16 or Romans 13:14 (or both verses).

7

The Fourth Virtue: Perseverance

And in your self-control, [add] perseverance.
—2 PETER 1:6

If it's difficult for adults to persevere at tasks, imagine the challenges for your children. Learning to "hang in there" and be patient is difficult when you're young. Our son David learned the challenge of perseverance a few years ago while trying to make the high school basketball team. Years later, as a college student, David recalled the situation in a paper for his English class.

Basketball tryouts approached quickly my ninth grade year. As I searched for ways to impress the coaches those first few days of practice, I began to doubt myself and wonder if I was really skilled enough to make the team. Those feelings of doubt infiltrated my mind, and soon, those unbearable thoughts became reality. When I found that my name was not included on the team roster, I not only determined to make the team the following season, but to lead it. If I had known the time, practice, and commitment it would take to succeed, I would have given up then. But slowly, I pressed on.

Every weekday afternoon was spent in the weight room and outdoors running and practicing as the six-foot, 125-pound kid grew into a six-foot-three-inch, 180-pound upperclassman.

"MAKE THE STARTERS BETTER"

David joined the varsity team during his sophomore year and had some playing time. When his junior year came around, he was excited at his prospects. But just before the first game, the coach pulled him aside. He had not been satisfied with David's level of improvement during practice, and he handed him a piece of paper explaining his role on the team: "You will have limited playing time until your skill and athleticism improve. You also need to work harder in practice to make the *starters* better."

David described in his essay his responses to the note and the situation. We include it as a reminder of the frustrations and opportunities your children may have in learning to persevere. David's story also reminds us of the spiritual resources we can give our children to make them strong during those challenging times.

How could I react to a message like this? What benefit had it been to spend countless hours in the weight room and at practice to watch my teammates do well and try to make them better? Did I really want to play basketball anymore?

Our team had certain weight-lifting requirements that many of the players neglected. One day, I remember standing in the weight room after finishing a set of leg presses and looking around to find that I was the only one working out. Many of the players, instead, would regularly go to the Waffle House; they were the ones who got to play while I watched.

Driving home from the games, I would often find myself nearly weeping, trying to uncover a reason for this overwhelming hardship. I prayed that God would give me an answer, only to find that no immediate solution was attainable. Instead, a Scripture verse came to mind, and once I read it, I thought about it constantly.

"Humble yourselves under the mighty hand of God, that He may exalt you at the proper time, casting all your anxiety on Him, because

He cares for you" (1 Peter 5:6–7). Suddenly, I realized that my life was full of pride, and if I wanted to change as a player, I had to change as a person first. My attitude needed an adjustment. The pride that I possessed made me too concerned about how people perceived me or what they thought of me as a basketball player. I decided to focus on encouraging my teammates and looked for opportunities to act as a servant. I found that this was the key to remaining humble.

I had faith that God would protect me and provide strength at the proper time, but I knew that success would not come without hard work. Throughout the remainder of the season, I purposed in my heart to be a servant, an encouragement, and the hardest working player on the team because I knew that one day my opportunity would arrive. Watching the guys my own age playing well and excelling was no longer a problem for me.

I also discovered that in order to become a leader on the team, I had to be willing to undergo various tasks that none of the other players would do. At a sleep-over party, I awoke early, before anyone else, and left to go practice with another team. I spent hours on the weekends practicing and studying the game on my own. On several occasions I met with my coach in his office to discuss the steps I needed to take to significantly improve before my senior year.

That summer and fall preceding the season, I spent hours upon hours playing and practicing. In a typical day, I would shoot over 800 shots and then work out with weights for an hour and a half. My shooting improved tremendously; I had totaled over 25,000 shots, and had gained twenty additional pounds. I was also in prayerful thought over the two verses in 1 Peter (remembering to stay humble and encourage others).

David had what he called an "exciting senior year" as a basketball player. He was a starter; in fact, he was a team captain and met with the referees at center court before each game. In his final game he scored a game high 22 points. Later, at the postseason awards ceremony, David receive the Coaches Award.

David concluded his essay by describing another personal highlight at the ceremony:

I suddenly heard a teacher giving a speech on love and encouragement and concluded by announcing the winners of the Encouragement Award. This particular award is given to one guy and one girl from each class, and when I heard my name called, I was shocked. As I received the beautiful plaque and headed back to my seat, my basketball coach, who was also the school's athletic director, approached the stage to present an award.

"Every year we like to give an award for the most outstanding senior athlete," he began. "And this year's senior athlete is . . . David Harper." At first, the name did not register. When I had finally confirmed it in my mind, I rushed up to the stage into the arms of the man who had been my coach for the last three years, the man who would not believe in me until I believed in myself. And I could not have confidence until I learned to trust God and His Word. It took time for that self-confidence to develop, which would never have occurred without a changed heart. Throughout this troubling experience, I acquired a heart of love, encouragement, and perseverance that enabled me to grow in remarkable ways.

As we embraced on that stage, hearing the cheerful applause, I remembered the verse on which I had focused. God had exalted me at the proper time and had also turned my failure into a great lesson of success.

Of course, as parents you will persevere as much as your children. Many times you will face tribulation with your children and will need to add perseverance. Life would certainly be a lot easier if parents did not have to add for themselves—and their children—any more virtues to goodness, knowledge, and self-control. About the time you feel that your child is becoming adequate and equipped, the progress seems to stop.

Those setbacks can happen in many ways. One day everything seems to be going well, and the next day your daughter comes home upset that the other girls are talking behind her back, or your son was cut from the team during tryouts, or he or she has been unjustly treated.

Often, our children handle their tribulations better than we do; it is easy for us to overreact and mishandle even the slightest disruption of what we consider a normal life. However, it is those interruptions (being held back from our own desires) that God uses to test the focus of our hearts.

Perhaps the definition of *perseverance* in its original Greek can help shed light on this fourth virtue. Perseverance comes from the word *hupomone,* which means "a remaining behind, a patient enduring." Why would our children need to "remain behind" and "patiently endure" in order to have "true knowledge of Jesus Christ," which keeps us from stumbling? Let's try to understand it together.

MISTREATED AND FORGOTTEN

One of the greatest deceptions we all face is viewing tribulations as bad, even evil. We see persevering through trials as negative, but God views tribulations very differently. Remember Joseph in the Bible? For many years Joseph lived with brothers who treated him with disdain and jealousy. Eventually they trapped and sold him as a slave to be taken to Egypt.

However, Joseph became successful as overseer of the house of Potiphar, the captain of Pharaoh's bodyguard. It seemed his trials were over. But just as things seemed to be going well for Joseph, his faith was deeply tested. For resisting the sexual enticements of his boss's wife—for having self-control and not yielding to temptation—he wound up in prison. You would have thought that doing the right thing would have promised him immediate relief; however, Potiphar's wife falsely accused Joseph of attacking her, even though he had run from her sight. Now in prison, Joseph seemed forgotten.

Yet, the Lord had not forgotten him. God blessed Joseph with the correct interpretation of Pharaoh's dream, and consequently Joseph was made ruler over all of Egypt.

Later, Joseph would be the brother who would bring his family to Egypt during a great famine in the world. When Joseph was finally alone with his brothers, Scripture says that "he wept so loudly that the Egyptians heard it." When his brothers recognized him, they were dismayed to the point they could not answer, and Joseph responded,

*I am your brother Joseph, whom you sold into Egypt. Now
do not be grieved or angry with yourselves, because you sold
me here, for God sent me before you to preserve life . . .
[and] to preserve for you a remnant in the earth, and to keep
you alive by a great deliverance. Now, therefore, it was not
you who sent me here, but God; and He has made me
a father to Pharaoh and lord of all his household
and ruler over all the land of Egypt.*

GENESIS 45:4–5, 7–8

Later, after Joseph's father died and his brothers were afraid that
he might bear a grudge, "Joseph said to them, 'Do not be afraid, for
am I in God's place? As for you, you meant evil against me, but God
meant it for good in order to bring about this present result, to preserve many people alive'" (Genesis 50:19–20).

A PURPOSE IN PERSEVERING

Clearly, God has a good purpose in tribulations, and He blesses
those who persevere in adversity and trust Him as the sustainer.

Think of the time back in school when one of your teachers walked
into the classroom and said, "All right, class, put away your books, and
pull out a blank sheet of paper. This is a pop quiz over the material
we covered last week." Can you remember that sinking feeling that so
dramatically altered your demeanor—and just as the day was going so
well! All she had to say was, "pop quiz," and suddenly all you could
remember was how to spell "depression." What was it about those
tests that depressed us so? Was it because we had not studied and were
afraid of failing? Was it because we considered it a disruption from
our regular chats and note writing to our neighbors? Whatever it was,
it seemed like a huge interruption and waste of good time.

Perseverance is much like a pop quiz. We neither ask to persevere nor do we expect to. But the Lord periodically gives us a pop
test to see if we have been paying attention, to see if we will be obe-

dient to Him regardless of the circumstance, regardless of its duration or severity. It is a true test of our faithfulness, and the Lord uses it to see what is in our hearts. If we have been hiding His Word in our heart and paying close attention to His voice, we will pass the test.

THE VALUE OF PATIENTLY ENDURING

In our fast-pace culture, we have a hard time valuing a "patient enduring" or "remaining behind." In a recent commercial, a man waited to download information on his computer. While he waited, he cooked, washed his hair, and rolled around in his chair doing various tasks. Most viewers laugh at the commercial, but it is true. We have little tolerance when it comes to having to wait or remain behind; we want to fill our time, to do things now. That inability to be patient is particularly true when we see others so far ahead of us.

Our children need to know that this life is not about them (as much as they are a wonderful gift to us). It is about knowing Jesus, and living for Him. We must be confident that tribulation is for our good and for our children's good. That is why Scripture tells us to rejoice and consider it all joy because our testing causes us to persevere. "Knowing that the testing of your faith produces endurance. And let endurance have its perfect result, so that you may be perfect and complete, lacking in nothing" (James 1:3–4).

A group from our church once reported on a mission trip to Russia. At one point they were traveling to a particular church to distribute Bibles. It had been snowing, and it took them a while to reach the church. When they finally arrived, the smiling faces of men, women, teenagers, and children, who were bundled up in coats and scarves, cheerfully greeted them. They had been waiting for over five hours in a church with no heat to receive Bibles from their American visitors.

On another occasion, the American visitors came to a nursing home. When they entered one room, the woman sat up in bed and began to cry very loudly and speak something in her Russian language. When they asked what she had said, someone told them, "My husband said before he died that one day the Americans would bring Jesus to us.

They had learned the blessing of persevering. As parents we need to learn that too.

God will take our children through whatever is necessary to conform them to His image. We must look at perseverance as a positive virtue that is necessary before our children can add godliness (a virtue that causes Jesus to say, "Well done, good and faithful servant! You have been faithful" [Matthew 25:21 NIV]).

HINDRANCES TO PERSEVERING

Before we present some steps that will enable you to help your children persevere, we ask that you consider some ways you and your spouse may be keeping your children from persevering. The next time a son or daughter encounters a trial or test, ask yourself these five questions:

1. Am I trying to control my child's happiness?
2. Am I being prideful? Is my self-image wrapped up in his or her success and achievements?
3. Am I losing my patience waiting for my child to persevere?
4. Am I being sensitive to the Holy Spirit and my child's spirit?
5. Am I too tired to help my child?

Perhaps you find yourself answering yes to several of these attitudes or conditions. We realize that parenting is demanding and at times tiring. If you feel that you have reached the "end of your rope," you need to seriously consider taking a respite. Get away by yourself if necessary. Have your spouse or a child-sitter watch the children for an afternoon, or together retreat for a day or weekend. There have been times that David has gone to a monastery across town to renew his mental, physical, and emotional strength. Right now, I am spending the week by myself at a nearby retreat center to write without distractions.

These hindrances are changeable; thank the Lord! So consider them before helping your child. Realize this, however: During the early years when your children are young, you will be the one persevering the most. This is God's way of preparing us to help them. Therefore, we need to practice and demonstrate these principles as well.

SEVEN STEPS FOR PERSEVERING

In high school and college, many students learned the benefits of reading "Cliff Notes," summaries and analyses of classic works of literature. After reading the particular book, the notes in the booklets helped them understand the work so they would be better prepared for a class discussion or an exam. When it comes to perseverance, here are the summary steps we have used time and time again with our children as well as with other youth we have worked with over the years. You could call them the "Cliff Notes" for helping your child pass the test. They are:

1. Be sensitive to their spirits.
2. Empathize without undermining authority.
3. Share similar examples with positive outcomes.
4. Take your children to the Word.
5. Help them catch a glimpse of God's purpose or future plan.
6. Pray with thanksgiving.
7. Trust God.

On page 136–7, we fill in each of the "Cliff Notes for Persevering" with specific ideas. But here are a couple of more ideas for notes two, six, and seven.

A couple of cautions on note (or step) two, "empathize without undermining authority." First, don't react defensively on behalf of your child when he or she is being corrected by an authority. For instance, don't rush to the school, grab the phone in haste, or make negative comments about the person or group of people involved. When we do that, we are teaching our child to blame others, hold grudges, and never take responsibility. Ultimately doing that will only cause the child to forgo the blessing associated with persevering. God wants to teach the child how to resolve conflict inwardly and learn something new about His Son, Jesus, in the process.

Second, when someone in authority has corrected your child and your son or daughter disputes the person's judgment, do not assume that your child is completely innocent. For that matter, do not place the blame solely on the child either. Simply listen. You may be thinking and planning what you want to say or do, but never verbalize them to your child. Be sensitive about when and how to get involved.

Cliff Notes for Persevering

Teaching your children to persevere is teaching them to trust God and learn patience when they feel falsely accused or frustrated by not receiving an answer or outcome in a timely or expected manner. Here are seven steps to help your children develop the virtue of perseverance.

1. Be sensitive to their spirits. Generally, you will be able to recognize when your children are facing a test or trial. To help you in being sensitive, ask your children, "What happened today at school?" or "What's wrong? I can tell that something is wrong. Do you feel frustrated or hurt about something?" Learn to hear words not spoken and see tears not cried. When you do, the child will open up eventually and express his grievances.
2. Empathize without undermining authority. Certainly you need to empathize with your children for the way they are feeling by saying things like, "I'm so sorry; I know that must have hurt your feelings" or, "I can understand how you would be upset about that." But it is unwise to undermine the authorities who are involved in their struggle, such as a teacher, coach, other parents, and friends for that matter.
3. Share similar examples with positive outcomes. If you do not have a similar story, use an example from someone else your children may know. Help them to see by the outcome of the test that "God Will Provide" for them as He did for you or for your friend. Hearing your story will help your children see the issues are similar, you understand to some extent their problems, and God honors their perseverance. This can give your children a determination to please Christ.
4. Take your children to the Word of God. His Word can speak in ways that we might not be able to. There are many wonderful Scriptures you can show during times of perseverance. (Scriptures your children can consult to remind them of our good God and great Savior who sustains at school, work, and in their relationships are shown in Resource Four.) Remember, the psalmist's refreshment found in the Word of God: "If Your law

had not been my delight, then I would have perished in my affliction. I will never forget Your precepts, for by them You have revived me" (Psalm 119:92–93).

5. Help them catch a glimpse of God's purpose or future plan. Once you have read the Word with them, help them to look beyond their immediate circumstances to sense God's purpose. We must remind them that "God causes all things to work together for good to those who love God" (Romans 8:28). Scripture also tells us that "Although He was a Son, He [Jesus] learned obedience from the things which He suffered" (Hebrews 5:8). Point out things they can learn from their situation—humility, gratitude, empathy, and leadership, to name a few.

6. Pray with thanksgiving. The most important aspect of your prayer should be *praise* for God and *thanksgiving* for what God will teach your child in his circumstance. Nothing improves our attitude like gratitude. Allow your child to pray as well. Suggest that he praise the Lord concerning his situation.

7. Encourage them to trust God for the outcome. Children need to be reassured that God will not allow anything to happen to them that is not for their good. The greatest way of doing this is for you to trust God yourself in everyday circumstances, especially when your child must persevere. When we recognize that perseverance is critical for our children to be able to understand and grow in the remaining virtues, we will help in setting the atmosphere of trust. Moreover, our children need to know that despite what happens in this life, God will reward them for their perseverance. (See, for example, Matthew 5:12, 43–46; 1 Timothy 4:8–10.)

When John David was persevering through his junior year of basketball, our hearts at times were breaking. At one game I had to leave and walk outside the gym to cry and pray. However, we never made negative comments about his coach or his playing skills to J. David. Toward the end of the season, David called the coach and made an appointment to visit with him. When he arrived, the coach began to brag on our son and his attitude. When David left he felt better about the coach and understood a little better about why J. David was not playing.

We understood that this was not just a test of endurance to see how patient J. David could be until he got to play. This was a test of attitude toward God to see if we would *all* trust Him by continuing to love, worship and obey Him regardless of the circumstance. To persevere to know Him better *in* this test, we had to direct J. David to the rest of the steps.

Concerning note (or step) six, "Pray with thanksgiving," remind your child of examples from the Word of God. The apostle Paul, for example, went through every imaginable tribulation you can think of (see 2 Corinthians 11:23–28); yet he wrote, "We also exult in our tribulations, knowing that tribulation brings about perseverance; and perseverance, proven character; and proven character, hope; and hope does not disappoint, because the love of God has been poured out within our hearts through the Holy Spirit who was given to us" (Romans 5:3–5).

This same Paul would later write, "In everything by prayer and supplication *with thanksgiving* let your requests be made known to God" (Philippians 4:6, italics added).

Concerning note (or step) seven, "Trust God," remember that seeing God work during the trial or suffering can give them confidence to endure. That was the case of a young pastor from Zimbabwe in prison. He wrote of his determination to persevere regardless of his circumstances:

> I'm part of a fellowship of the unashamed. I have the Holy Spirit power. The die has been cast. I have stepped over the line. The decision has been made—I'm a disciple of His. I won't look back, let up, slow down, back away, or be still. My past is redeemed; my present makes sense, my future secure. I'm finished and done with low living, sight walking, smooth knees, colorless dreams, tamed visions, worldly talking, cheap giving, and dwarfed goals. . . .
>
> My face is set, my gait is fast, my goal is heaven, my road is narrow, my way is rough, my companions few, my Guide reliable, my mis-

sion clear. I cannot be bought, compromised, detoured, lured away, turned back, deluded, or delayed. I will not flinch in the face of sacrifice, hesitate in the presence of the enemy, pander at the pool of popularity, or meander in the maze of mediocrity.

I won't give up, shut up, let up, until I have stayed up, stored up, prayed up, paid up, preached up for the cause of Christ. I am a disciple of Jesus Christ. I must go until He comes, give until I drop, preach until all know, and work until He stops me. And when He comes for His own, He will have no trouble recognizing me . . . my banner will be clearly visible and flying![1]

This confession was found pinned to his prison cell wall after he was martyred for his belief in Jesus Christ. He passed the test. Let us help our children learn to persevere on their own, for we do not know what this life holds. We must begin to point them towards eternity.

How do we do that? Let us be sensitive to their spirits, empathize without undermining authority, share similar examples with positive outcomes, take them to the Word, help them catch a glimpse of God's purpose or future plan, pray with thanksgiving, and trust God. In our lives there are two guarantees: Life is hard. God is sufficient!

F a n   t h e   F l a m e

1. Can you think of times when Jesus had to remain behind and patiently endure?

2. Perseverance is a pivotal virtue, and learning the virtue will have long-lasting effects. Identify some things your children can learn from perseverance that they cannot learn in any other way. What could happen if they did not learn to practice perseverance? What does God desire to teach us through persevering?

3. List the seven ways you will help your child to persevere, shown in the "Cliff Notes for Persevering." Now use a present situation in which one of your children, or spouse, is persevering, and make a plan for implementing each step.

4. As we help our children to persevere, consider another name of God, one that can reassure them that in Him a victorious outcome awaits. *El Shaddai* means "The All Sufficient One." It is the earliest recorded name for God (used in Genesis 17:1–3). Bible commentator Andrew Jukes describes the sufficiency of *El Shaddai* this way:

> The name *Shaddai* describes power, but it is the power, not of violence, but of all-bountifulness. *Shaddai* primarily means "breasted," being formed directly from the Hebrew word, *Shad,* that is, "the breast," or more exactly, a "woman's breast." Parkhurst thus explains the name: "Shaddai, one of the divine titles, meaning The Pourer or Shedder forth, that is, of blessings, temporal and spiritual. This is 'El Shaddai,' the 'Pourer-forth,' who pours Himself out for His creatures; who gives them His lifeblood; who 'sheds forth His Spirit,' and says, 'Come unto Me and drink': and 'Open thy mouth wide and I will fill it': and who thus, by sacrifice of Himself, gives Himself and His very nature to those who will receive Him, that thus His perfect will may be accomplished in them."[2]

This is a name we must treasure. The next time your child must persevere, how will you encourage him in God's name?

5. Read 1 Peter 4:12–19. What are the wonderful truths from this passage that you can pass on to your children?

The Big Question

How will perseverance help your child know God better?

Family Activities

Read or tell the story of Shadrach, Meshach, and Abed-nego (Daniel 3) to your children. Then have them look again at verses 17 and 18. Discuss the fact that they were choosing to worship and serve God, knowing that He could deliver them. But "even if He does not . . . we are not going to serve your gods or worship the golden image" (verse 18). Ask them what happened as a result of their passion for God. (Also read through Daniel 4:1–3.) Finally, ask them to explain the value of having close Christian friends.

Sit down and put a 500-piece puzzle together with your children (more or less depending on their ages) Even if you have to leave it for days, come back to it periodically and work on it until it is finished. Afterward, ask them about their teamwork: "What can this help teach?"

Memory Verse

Have your children memorize James 1:2–4 or 1:12.

8

The Fifth Virtue: Godliness

And in your perseverance, [add] godliness.
—2 PETER 1:6

When Kris Tuck died in Botswana, Africa, during a mission trip with Campus Outreach, no one grieved more than our son, David, who was Kris's best friend in high school. They had even planned to be in each other's weddings. David and Kris were accountability partners and prayed together several times a week during lunch. Kris was on fire for God, and nothing was going to keep him from living to please God in all he did.

But before the ninth grade, Kris would have nothing to do with God. He was a self-confessed "wild man." His parents were so concerned about his grades and his involvement in the wrong things that they put him in a Christian school. It happened to be the one that our children attended. One day during chapel, Kris gave his life to the Lord. He started attending church, as well as an early morning Bible study before school. Kris began to not only grow in leaps and bounds spiritually, but he also became a vital spiritual leader in the school. His passion for God was contagious!

If someone had a problem, Kris would pray with them. He learned quickly what it meant to give himself as a living sacrifice for others.

In college he became involved in Campus Outreach and participated in various mission trips every summer. "I want to lead people to Jesus Christ," Kris told his parents before leaving for Africa. His greatest passion was to know Christ and to make Him known. Kris grew to know Jesus so well that he could say as Paul said, "For to me, to live is Christ and to die is gain" (Philippians 1:21). And in the process of doing just that, Kris "gained" Christ when a couple of donkeys crossing the road caused their vehicle to overturn. Three girls were injured; Kris died.

In the words of his spiritual mentor, Barry St. Clair, Kris could say, "Mission accomplished!" At Kris's funeral, at least twenty-four people who filled out cards received Jesus Christ that day, including his brother.

We must not give up hope for our children's spiritual growth. Kris's parents did not.

As children and young people grow in their walk with the Lord, they will move from being focused more on themselves to being focused more on God. The truth of the matter is that most people bail out way before they get to this virtue. Perseverance paves the way to godliness, but many people give up in the persevering process. They invent ways to cope and manipulate on their own rather than fully trust God.

The same is true in parenting. Rather than allowing their children to persevere through difficulties, parents tend to bail them out of trouble. For example, if their child is struggling with a situation, the parents blame the teacher, the principal, the coach, the preacher, the music leader, the friend, the neighbor, or anyone else who can be blamed. They move from school to school, from neighborhood to neighborhood, from church to church, avoiding conflicts and difficulties, never persevering long enough to get to the virtue of godliness.

When our children were young, there were certain neighborhood friends that we felt were not good influences on our children. For years David and I tried hard to "pray them away." When it became obvious that they were going nowhere, we decided to change our attitude and use it as a training ground for our children to learn godliness by being able to stand against negative influences. They learned to be friends with them, while at the same time trying to influence them rather than be influenced by them.

Sometimes our children would come into the house telling us that these particular boys were cursing, or saying that there was no God, or being destructive, or looking at bad magazines. We had many family discussions about the best way to respond to those situations. As a result, they began to develop their spiritual muscles for godliness. And so we stress the importance of parents being available to their children so that they can guide them through these situations. Looking back, we see that God answered our prayers differently than what we expected.

GOOD WORSHIP, SPIRITUAL WORSHIP

Our children were learning at a young age what it meant to present their bodies to God as "a living . . . sacrifice" (Romans 12:1). What does it mean to present our bodies as "living sacrifices"? It means that something has to die. That something is our children's own will so that they can find and follow God's will. This is their "spiritual service of worship."

Significantly, the word *godliness* in 2 Peter 1:6 comes from the Greek word *eusebeia,* which is composed of two root words: *eu,* meaning "good; well" (the same word that Jesus used when He said, "Well done, good and faithful servant!" in Matthew 25:23 NIV), and *sebo,* meaning "to worship." Therefore, a helpful definition of godliness would be "worshiping God in a way that pleases Him."

This spiritual worship of Romans 12:1 reflects the service that the high priests formerly performed. They would sacrifice a chosen animal at the entrance of the tabernacle or temple, cleanse their hands in the laver for their purification, then they would enter the Holy Place and light the sacred oil lamps, and tend to the loaves of bread. They would then enter behind the veil to burn sacred incense and sprinkle the blood of the animal on the mercy seat. This is what the Lord required as an acceptable service of worship.

However, once a person enters into a personal relationship with Jesus, the Holy Spirit comes into the person's life, and one's body becomes the temple. The individual then can become a living sacrifice. When one sacrifices his or her own will on the altar, the person will purify and cleanse the heart, turning up the lamp of the Holy Spirit, and take in His Word (the bread). He or she then has intimate access to the Father. This is our spiritual service of worship. It is a sacred service that we do for Him, and He reveals to us His perfect will.

What greater motive do we have for teaching our children godliness? More than anything we should want them to know and follow God's *perfect will.* In the next verse Paul explained the "nuts and bolts" of training them in godliness (or "good worship"). "And do not be conformed to this world, but be transformed by the renewing of your mind, that you may prove what the will of God is, so that which is good and acceptable and perfect" (Romans 12:2).

Hence, when situations come up like wrong influences in the neighborhood, parents can help their children to be transformed, by renewing their minds with Scripture so that they will not be conformed to this world. In that way they learn in everyday life to sacrifice the attractions of the world to follow something better—God's perfect will. As preacher and author Charles Stanley told his son growing up, "Andy, whatever you do, don't miss God's perfect will."

Intimate access with the Father is our joy. And to have such closeness to God we must engage in worship, indicates devotional writer Dan DeHaan. "Why should we worship God? God knows that it is in the act of worship that He draws near to us, communicating His person to us, and sharing His secrets with us."[1]

Such intimate access is part of our spiritual service of worship. The other part is learning and teaching our children to become "a living and holy sacrifice." Several years ago we learned how such sacrifices are acts of spiritual worship. In the neighborhood where our children grew up, all the parents agreed to a fair rule: If one child broke another child's toy, the offender had to pay for the toy. One day the son of a neighbor who lived across the street, Stephen, and another boy, Sam, found Daniel's "match box" cars on a stump behind the house. Since the toy cars were in Sam's yard, the boys decided to crush all of them.

When our neighbor found out what her son had done, she brought him over to apologize and pay for the cars. We listened and forgave. Then I said, "That's OK, Stephen; don't worry about it. We don't want you to pay for them; we forgive you, and we appreciate your coming over to apologize." Stephen's mother never forgot that. Our friendship has grown dear over the years. I am grateful to God for helping me to do His perfect will that day—a little *sacrifice* that *proved* to have a big impact.

When we give up or sacrifice something in honor of God's will, we are not really losing anything. In fact, author C. S. Lewis suggested that true pleasures come from God, and that evil is just a distortion of the good thing that God created. In Lewis's book *The Screwtape Letters,* a senior demon, writing to a demon in training, explains their need to distort God's good creation of pleasure: "Never forget that when we are dealing with any pleasure in its healthy and normal and satisfying form, we are, in a sense, on the enemy's [God's] ground . . . All we can do is to encourage the humans to take the pleasures which our enemy has produced, at times, or ways, or in degrees, which He has forbidden."

Then Uncle Screwtape, the senior demon, concludes, "Hence, we always try to work our way from the natural condition of any pleasure to that which is least natural . . . an ever increasing craving for an ever diminishing pleasure is the formula."[2]

Such distorted pleasures appeal as much to parents as to children. As a result, the attractions of the world, when we give them up, appear to be a substantial sacrifice. In reality we are obtaining something that is much better—God's good and wise gifts. As James wrote, "Every perfect gift is from above, coming down from the Father of lights" (1:17). When we enjoy God's gifts, we are brought closer to Him.

Later on, Screwtape chastised Wormwood, noting the good and perfect gifts God offers to the creatures He created:

And now for your blunders. . . . You first of all allowed the patient to read a book he really enjoyed, because he enjoyed it and not to make clever remarks about it to his new friends. In the second place, you allowed him to walk down to the old mill and have tea there—a walk through the country he really likes, and taken alone. . . . Remember always, that He really likes the little vermin [people], and sets an absurd value on the distinctness of every one of them. When He talks of them losing their selves, He only means abandoning the clamor of self-will; once they have done that, He really gives them back all their personality, and boasts that when they are wholly His they will be more themselves than ever.[3]

The act of worship also enables us to see God as He really is. During a 1994 Promise Keepers conference in Atlanta, Jack Hayford described worship this way: "Worship is the magnifying glass that ignites the power of God in our lives." When we worship God we are empowered to obey Him in the broad perspective of our whole life. Worship is not just a matter of singing praise songs, even though such praise is important. Worship involves everything we say, think, or do. Sacrifice reveals our deep-down attitudes and motives for doing everything.

THE SPIRITUAL VERSUS THE SECULAR

It is very easy for us to compartmentalize our lives between certain activities we deem to be spiritual and other activities we deem to be merely secular. But the spiritual dimension should and can influence every element of our lives. I (David) learned that truth in 1994, and it changed me forever in this area of godliness. I was at my office desk early in the morning, staring through the window into the darkness and pleading with God.

"Lord, I really want to know what You want. I don't want to leave until You reveal exactly what I need to do. Do You want me to quit what I'm doing? Do You want me to go to seminary? Do You want me to go to the mission field? Whatever You want, I am willing."

To give you a little background, my associates and I had developed a financial services practice and had been in that business for seventeen years. For much of that time, I had wondered if this was what I was really supposed to be doing or something else. Also, Anne and I and some friends had just completed the last section in a three-year program on apologetics and spiritual disciplines, offered through Ravi Zacharias International Ministries. The last session dealt with discovering one's spiritual gifts and passion in order to fulfill God's calling in life.

Now, as I prayed, the Lord brought to mind the Scripture passage where an imprisoned John the Baptist sent his disciples to Jesus to ask if He was the Messiah, or should he look for someone else (see Matthew 11:2–3). I wondered why that Scripture came to my mind. Then I looked at Jesus' response in Matthew 11:4–5 NIV: "Go back and report to John what you hear and see: The blind receive sight . . ." In other words, Jesus was telling them to examine the evidence that demonstrated he was, in fact, the Messiah.

Then it dawned on me, John's disciples were asking a similar question to what I was asking. "Is this it, or am I to do something else?" Then the Lord spoke in my mind. "I have gifted you and strategically placed you exactly where I want you to be." What a relief it was to know this!

I had tended to look at my business as being a secular activity, but as I examined the evidence of where I was having the most spiritual impact with people outside the faith; it was with people with whom I had a business relationship.

I began to see that the marketplace of business was a tremendous opportunity to influence people for Christ. I remember saying to myself, "OK, if this is it, what should my business look like?" Another question came to mind: "If my business were to be exactly as it ought to be, what would that look like?" Simply continuing to ask that question began to have a powerful influence on my business.

For example, the Scriptures indicate we are to "proclaim the excellencies of Him who has called you" and to "keep [our] behavior excellent among the Gentiles, so that . . . they may . . . glorify God in the day of visitation" (1 Peter 2:9, 12). My focus began to shift from an emphasis on making a profit to excellence in service. Over time, this has brought a competitive advantage for our business in the marketplace. From this, I coined the term *market faith,* which means focusing on excellence to such an extent for the client that you forget about your personal interest.

Clearly, the Scriptures were reminding me that the spiritual dimension of my life can and should guide the secular aspects. Eventually, the theme of accountability from Scripture would become a greater priority for me. Recently, I have acquired three partners with the idea that we would provide accountability for each other from a biblical perspective. We developed our business plan with all these scriptural principles in mind. Even our name, *Executive Resources, Inc.,* was designed to communicate these concepts.

From that point on, I began to see business as a ministry that had equal weight to any other spiritual activity. As a matter of fact, work, playing baseball, taking your wife on a date, driving in your car, etc., have the same spiritual significance as to what we normally consider to be spiritual—going to church, reading your Bible, praying, and sharing your faith. I feel it is important that parents with careers acknowledge the lordship of Christ in order to have the balance between providing for the family and being available to the family.

OUR CHILDREN AND
THE SPIRITUAL VERSUS THE SECULAR

It is also easy for children to compartmentalize the spiritual and the secular. How do we keep our sons and daughters from falling into this trap of dividing the two? Children should be taught that playing with friends, cleaning up their rooms, setting the table, taking out the trash, riding their bicycle, if done for the Lord, all have spiritual significance. Such activities have the same spiritual significance as saying their prayers, reading the Bible, and going to church.

Encourage your children to look for opportunities to include the spiritual in every activity. For instance, Daniel ran track in high school, and he decided before every race he would shake everyone's hand and say, "God bless you; have a great race." Daniel won the county championship in the 110-meter high hurdles and placed third at the state meet. With his giving of these blessings and in his performances, we feel that he was able to influence people for Christ in a positive way.

Every thought, word, or deed that is done to the glory of God is an act of worship. This is godliness. On top of all this, God is pleased when we worship Him. This was on Paul's heart when he prayed,

We have not ceased to pray for you and to ask that you may be
filled with the knowledge of His will in all spiritual wisdom
and understanding, so that you will walk in a manner worthy
of the Lord, to please Him in all respects, bearing fruit
in every good work and increasing in the knowledge
of God; *strengthened with all power, according to His glori-*
ous might, for the attaining of all steadfastness and patience;
joyously giving thanks to the Father, who has qualified us to
share in the inheritance of the saints in Light.

COLOSSIANS 1:9–12; emphasis added

We love praying those verses for our children.

TELLING OUR CHILDREN WHO GOD IS

Jesus said in John 4:23 that "true worshipers will worship the
Father in spirit and truth; for such people the Father seeks to be His
worshipers."

What does it mean to worship God in spirit and in truth? To worship God in spirit means that we recognize that God Himself is the
one who enables us to worship. He is initiating the whole process,
giving us the desire and power to please Him in worship. To worship God in truth means focusing our attention, as Francis Schaeffer
stated, on "The God who is there."

Our culture suggests that God is whoever we believe Him to be
because in reality He is just a figment of our imagination anyway.
From time to time, I will hear people say, "My God is not a god who
would do such and such," as if what they say about Him defines who
He really is. Of course, the God of the Bible is different than that.
God is, and the only way we know about Him, is that He chooses
to reveal who He is.

If our culture is confused, you know this must be confusing to
children. The Bible clearly reveals the truth of who God is. The following chart compares common false conceptions of God to the true
reality of God.

UNDERSTANDING WHO GOD IS

FALSE STATEMENTS

- God is limited.

- We can hide from God.

- God does not take sin seriously.

- God is too busy to be concerned about "small things."

- God is an impersonal force like "Mother Nature."

- If God knows everything about the future, everything is predetermined; therefore, He gives us no choice.

- God changes just like everything else.

TRUE STATEMENTS

- God is unlimited. He knows everything.

- God is everywhere. There is no hiding from God.

- God is just and moral. He takes sin so seriously that Jesus was crucified to pay the penalty of sin.

- God is all-powerful and is concerned about the smallest to the greatest issues.

- God is personal. The Father, Son, and Holy Spirit are three persons, yet one in essence.

- God is eternal. Everything is present to Him. His foreknowledge does not take away man's free will.

- God is perfect. He cannot change.

Notice the first false concept, "God is limited." Parents at times tend to think of God in terms of very narrow slots in our lives, such as church activities, Bible reading, and prayer. We may even believe that God shouldn't be discussed in public. However, when we understand who God is, we will recognize He deserves to be a part of every aspect of our lives. We and our children will be ready to worship Him.

If we do not worship God, we will worship something or someone else. Everyone worships something whether they realize it or not. If it is not God, it is themselves, a musician, an athlete, their car, their girlfriend or boyfriend, their work, their house, money, sports, nature, or other false gods. Clearly God has placed in us the desire to worship. Who—or what—will it be? God desires that we come to know and worship only Him, the true God. And it is important that we have the right concept of who He really is. When we know the true God and give Him right worship, He strongly supports us (see 2 Chronicles 16:9).

ABRAHAM WORSHIPED GOD

Real spiritual worship involves sacrifice, as Paul noted in his call that followers of Christ be "living sacrifices." Nowhere in Scripture is the call to sacrifice more clearly shown than in Abraham's encounter with God on Moriah in Genesis 22. "Now it came about after these things, that God tested Abraham. . . . 'Take now your son, your only son, whom you love, Isaac, and go to the land of Moriah, and offer him there as a burnt offering on one of the mountains of which I will tell you.'"

Can you imagine? No warning or explanation whatsoever! Abraham, as far as we know, never even questioned God. The next verse says, "So Abraham rose early in the morning and saddled his donkey, and took two of his young men with him and Isaac his son; and he split the wood for the burnt offering, and arose and went to the place of which God had told him." Verse 5 is significant: "And Abraham said to his [servants], 'Stay here with the donkey, and I and the lad will go over there; and we will *worship* and return to you'" (italics added). Worship was always Abraham's motive in offering a sacrifice.

Then Abraham demonstrated his faith when Isaac asked, "'My father! ... Behold, the fire and the wood, but where is the lamb for the burnt offering?' Abraham said, 'God [*Elohim*, "the Creator, the mighty Three in One"] will provide for Himself the lamb for the burnt offering, my son'" (verses 7–8).

Abraham continued the preparation. Finally, he grabbed the knife, ready to sacrifice his beloved son. Then the angel of the Lord (Jehovah) called to him.

"Abraham! ... Do not stretch out your hand against the lad, and do nothing to him; for now I know that you fear God, since you have not withheld your son, your only son, from Me." Then Abraham raised his eyes and looked, and behold, behind him a ram caught in the thicket by his horns; and Abraham ... offered him up for a burnt offering in the place of his son. Abraham called the name of that place, The Lord Will Provide [Jehovah-Jireh].

VERSES 11–14

Abraham passed the test because he was willing to give up everything to love, worship, and obey God. Such faith—and such worship—has its reward. The angel of the Lord subsequently told Abraham,

---

"By Myself I have sworn, declares the Lord, because you have done this thing and have not withheld your son, your only son, indeed I will greatly bless you, and I will greatly multiply your seed as the stars of the heavens and as the sand which is on the seashore; and your seed shall possess the gate of their enemies. In your seed all the nations of the earth shall be blessed, because you have obeyed My voice."

VERSES 16–18

In this classic chapter of worship, Genesis 22, there are three words that God uses for the first time in the Bible: *love, worship,* and *obeyed.* From this point on, these three words become the focal point of God's message throughout Scripture. Our children will discover that if they are willing to sacrifice their own desires—whether popularity, possessions, position, and even family—to love, worship, and obey God, they will eventually learn that intimacy with God is more important than anything else.

Fan the Flame

1. If your child were to ask you, "Why was I born and what is my purpose for living?" what would you say? (See Isaiah 43:7 and Revelation 4:11 for help.)

2. In light of your answer to number one, what might you pray for your children and what would be the benefits? (Reflect upon Colossians 1:9–12.)

3. Since godliness (a worship that pleases God) involves sacrifice, identify one way you can help your children learn to make these sacrifices in which God delights: "your bodies as a living and holy sacrifice, acceptable to God" (Romans 12:1); "Loyalty. . . . and in the knowledge of God" (Hosea 6:6); "Gratitude" (Hebrews 12:28); "Praise to God" (Hebrews 13:15); "Doing good and sharing" (Hebrews 13:16); "Obey[ing] your leaders . . . . with joy" (Hebrews 13:17).

4. Describe how you will teach your children the need to worship God in all that they do, rather than making the spiritual a separate compartment from the secular.

5. Paul wrote that "godliness actually is a means of great gain when accompanied by contentment. For we have brought nothing into the world, so we cannot take anything out of it either" (1 Timothy 6:6–7). Why does contentment need to accompany godliness? How might you teach contentment to your children?

The Big Question

How will godliness help your child to know God better?

Family Activities

Read Jeremiah 9:23–24 to your family. Ask them to name the three things in which people tend to boast. Discuss the tendencies that they and you might have to boast in the wrong things. Then ask them to tell you what God prefers that they boast about. Lastly, ask them to name the things that God mentions that He wants us to know about Him.

Second Timothy 2 can keep you busy for weeks in pulling out truths for family devotions. Choose several verses at a time and try to be creative in your teaching. It is best if you can plan your devotional times early in the day rather than waiting until you are too tired to decide what to read and share. For example, discuss how they can be "teachers," "soldiers," "athletes," "farmers," and "workers" (verses 1–6, 15). Or, use a small "vessel" to teach confession and repentance (verses 20–21).

Learn to laugh, make mistakes, and have fun! Make your own Play-Doh. In a large pot mix: 2 cups plain flour, 2 cups water, 2 tablespoons oil, 1 cup salt, and 4 teaspoons cream of tartar. Stir together over medium heat until it becomes like dough. Let cool and add food coloring. Or make finger paint with flour, enough water to make a smooth paste, and food coloring. Spread out sheets of paper and allow your children to be creative!

Memory Verse

Have your children memorize 1 Timothy 4:7b–8. Young children may memorize just the last part of verse 7.

9

The Sixth Virtue: Brotherly Kindness

And in your godliness, [add] brotherly kindness.
—2 PETER 1:7

To millions, Mother Teresa was the epitome of the virtue *brotherly kindness,* which is mentioned in 2 Peter 1:7 as the sixth virtue. In her Nobel Prize acceptance speech, she told of this experience of someone else who demonstrated great kindness:

> I had the most extraordinary experience with a Hindu family who had eight children. A gentleman came to our house, and said: "Mother Teresa, there is a family with eight children; they have not eaten for so long; do something." So, I took some rice, and I went there immediately. And I saw the children, their eyes shining with hunger. I don't know if you have ever seen hunger. But I have seen it very often. And she [the Hindu mother] took the rice, she divided the rice, and she went out. When she came back, I asked: "Where did you go, what did you do?" And she gave me a very simple answer: "They are hungry also." What struck me most was that she knew—and who are they? A Muslim family—and she knew. I didn't bring more rice that evening because I

wanted them to enjoy the joy of sharing. But there were those children radiating joy, sharing the joy with their mother because she had
the love to give. And you see, this is where love begins—at home.[1]

Can you imagine sharing *all* that you have with neighbors who
have different beliefs, being sensitive to the point that you *know* their
needs? We hardly take time to notice when our close Christian brothers and sisters are in need. Yet, what an example we set for our children when we are kind to others. It must offend the Lord when we
are not, for He is the One who said, "To the extent that you did not
do it [feed, clothe, visit] to one of the least of these, you did not do
it to Me" (Matthew 25:45).

KEEPING *CHRISTIAN*

I am painfully reminded of a time when one of Daniel's elementary school friends, Christian, began to come home with him about
three days a week. Christian lived with his father and stepmother; his
mother lived in California, but because she believed that he would
receive a better education here, she let him stay with his father.

Daniel felt sorry for Christian, knowing that he would be home
alone on those days when his father and stepmother worked, so he
invited him to our house. I was happy at first; Christian was a precious boy, sweet and well mannered. However, I began to slowly resent not having my time alone with Daniel when he would come
home from school. I even began to worry about having enough food
for dinner if Christian's dad was late in picking him up. His name
was Christian, but he did not know the Lord and I was certainly not
influencing him by my attitude.

A couple months passed, and one day I was praying with my "Moms
In Touch" group when I felt a heavy conviction that I needed to demonstrate brotherly kindness to this young boy. I realized at that moment
how much God desired to extend His love to Christian, and that He
had chosen us to demonstrate His love and acceptance. Becoming a sub-
stitute mom for him became a huge desire of mine. God had spoken
to me so clearly that I resolved to say yes to his mother if she ever called
to officially ask me to keep him every afternoon.

As the Lord would have it, that afternoon I received a phone call from California. It was his mother. She described how Christian loved coming to our house and how burdened she was for him and that she hoped in the near future to have him come to California. She also asked if Christian could continue coming to our house three days a week until the end of the school year. I was delighted that God had prepared me for that moment when I would be thrilled to say yes.

Looking back, I realize how brief that time was—just a small window of opportunity. I am not sure how much we affected Christian's life before he moved to California to be with his mother. However, I know I was sad when he left. I still find myself missing him and wishing we had spent more time with him. We do not have long to influence others for Christ. Sometimes we have only a few minutes; sometimes we are blessed with years. But how we spend our time has eternal significance.

The Greek rendering for brotherly kindness is *philadelphia,* meaning "the love of brothers." The root word, *philos,* is translated as "beloved, dear, friendly."

The first five virtues have for the most part been self-focused. God has been teaching us much about Himself by exposing our own needs and inadequacies. We have looked *up,* and we have looked *in.* Now, through the Holy Spirit, it is time to look *out,* to become other-focused. As adults, we have lived enough years to know that it is difficult to love others and consider their needs when we have not learned how to deal with our own. That is why Peter waits until now to instruct us that "in [our] godliness, [we should add] brotherly kindness."

God's divine nature is one of unity; therefore, practicing goodness, knowledge, self-control, perseverance, and godliness prepares us to look beyond ourselves to our brothers in Christ and to a desperate world of people dying spiritually from a lack of knowledge of the Lord.

BROTHERLY KINDNESS: A RADICAL WAY TO LOVE

Before Jesus was crucified, He explained to His disciples that when He was gone they would need to be responsible for one very important duty, to "love one another even as I have loved you" (John

13:34). The love that Jesus had in mind was not what they were accustomed to. It begins with a brotherly kindness that is radical. In His Sermon on the Mount (Matthew 5–7), He described brotherly kindness in acts of love:

"Everyone who is angry with his brother shall be guilty" (5:22).

"If . . . your brother has something against you, . . go . . . [and] be reconciled to [him]" (5:23–24).

"Make friends quickly with your opponent at law" (5:25).

"Whoever slaps you on your right cheek, turn the other to him also" (5:39).

"Whoever forces you to go one mile, go with him two" (5:41).

"Love your enemies and pray for those who persecute you" (5:44).

"If you do not forgive others, then your Father will not forgive your transgressions" (6:15).

"Do not judge so that you will not be judged" (7:1).

COMPONENTS OF BROTHERLY KINDNESS: ACCEPTANCE

Brotherly kindness is a great means of influence, not only among other Christians but also among nonbelievers with whom we come in contact. Such kindness will also impress our children with how God works in our lives, and provide a model of how they are to live. Here are three components that we believe are very important in helping to teach *brotherly kindness* to our children: acceptance, availability, and accountability.

First, we need to teach our children to have a spirit of *acceptance*. If our children can learn to accept others just the way they are, without "judging the book by the cover," they win the awesome privilege of demonstrating God's acceptance for them—just the way they are. How can our children grow up sharing their faith with anyone if they have not first learned to have a spirit of acceptance?

We need to be clear, at this point, not to confuse acceptance with the modern definition of tolerance. In his book *The New Tolerance,* Josh McDowell indicated that the original definition of tolerance was more like acceptance. By acceptance, we mean that we should accept the person, but we are not required to accept the actions and values of that person. But in recent years, tolerance has come to mean accepting their actions and values as equal to your own. Our children need to know that by accepting others (faults and all) they have an opportunity to be an influence for Christ; they can open the door to a relationship that can influence the person toward Christ. They need not, indeed they should not, accept the person's values when different from their own. Our children can accept others and act in a friendly manner—even if they do not like the things they do.

Look at the life of Jesus and you will notice that He fully accepted everyone He met. His hope was to affect their life eternally—and He did. What He did not tolerate, however, were the obstinate, hard-hearted, proud religious leaders whom Satan used to work against the truth. Notice some of the people that Jesus accepted and how His kindness affected them:

- Jesus chose a dishonest tax collector, Matthew, as one of His twelve disciples. What effect did this have on Matthew? He not only followed Jesus to the end, but he also penned the most detailed account of all the Gospels. Matthew lived his life for Jesus and later gave his life for Jesus.
- Jesus befriended and healed Mary Magdalene of seven demons. She, along with several other women, contributed to the support of Jesus' ministry out of their own private means, and followed Him all the way to the cross (Matthew 27:55; Luke 8:2–3).
- The first person to whom Jesus ever revealed Himself was a Samaritan woman who was living in adultery. Jewish men were not to talk to women in public, especially not Samaritans, who were part Jew and part Gentile through intermarriage. His disciples marveled that He had been speaking with the woman. What was the effect? "From that city many of the Samaritans believed in [Jesus] because of the word of the woman who testified" (John 4:39).
- The Roman centurion who was present at the crucifixion of Jesus heard Jesus say, "Father, forgive them; for they do not know what they are doing" (Luke 23:34). No doubt, Jesus' words gave grace and healing to this leader. What was the effect of Jesus' kindness? Upon Jesus' surrendering His Spirit and dying, the

Gospel writer Luke recorded, "When the centurion saw what had happened, he began praising God, saying, 'Certainly this man was innocent'" (Luke 23:47).

The list is too numerous to describe all the people whom Jesus influenced because of His willingness to accept the unacceptable and forgive the unforgivable. Sometimes we find it hard to accept another person because deep down we are harboring bitterness and resentment about something that person did to us. Nonetheless, Jesus has much to say about forgiveness.

ACCEPTANCE AND FORGIVENESS

In one of His parables Jesus explained the importance of forgiveness. When Peter came to Jesus and asked, "Lord, how often shall my brother sin against me and I forgive him? Up to seven times?" Jesus answered, "I do not say to you, up to seven times, but up to seventy times seven" (Matthew 18:21–22). In other words, Peter was to forgive each transgression, every time.

Jesus then told Peter the parable of a forgiving king who forgave a servant a large debt. The servant, however, then refused to forgive a fellow slave a debt and had him imprisoned.

If your child has wronged another, help him to ask forgiveness in the right manner. Similarly, if your child has suffered wrongly, help him to grant forgiveness to the offender. Forgiveness is a critical part of acceptance. Our goal in teaching forgiveness is for our children to learn that regardless of who was wronged, they should seek to make things right. Seeking to make things right is brotherly kindness at its best. Tell your children that it is not always the *wrong* one who should ask for forgiveness, but the *strong* one.

When our boys were young and would occasionally mistreat Lauren, they would quickly and flippantly say, "Sorry, Lauren," and think that was sufficient. It was not. They had to be trained to say, "I'm sorry; would you forgive me?" Teach the one responding to say, "I forgive you." How often do you hear those words? Yet this demonstrates to others God's forgiveness without hesitation when we come to Him with a repentant heart.

Never allow unforgiveness to go unchecked. In Ephesians 4:26–27, Paul warned that we are not to go to bed at night with unresolved anger because this gives the devil an opportunity to set up a stronghold. Unforgiveness can poison a marriage, cripple the relationship between parent and child, stagnate a friendship, and ultimately destroy the work of God. Some people carry bitterness for years while it eats away at their health and sanity. That is Satan's delight.

When Susie, age thirteen, was persevering to have friendships in middle school, her mother shared with her the steps for persevering (shown in chapter 7). Her mom, Linda, told Susie about her own similar high school experiences—about rejection and even taunting. Despite the fact that Linda had felt innocent of wrongdoing, she still had harbored unforgiveness for many years toward the girls who had mistreated her. "The girls who were unkind to me never seemed to be remorseful. And even though I tried to be kind and forgiving, and even pray for them, I quietly harbored bitterness that I carried over into my adult years."

Linda told her daughter that ten years after she graduated she called one of the girls (symbolically representing *the group*) and said, "I just wanted to ask you to forgive me for not being a better friend to you in high school." (When you must be the strong one, do not point the blame; confess *only* where you have been wrong.)

"You didn't do anything wrong," the girl responded, sounding amazed by the call.

"Well, I don't want anything to stand in the way of my walk with the Lord, and it would make me feel better if you would forgive me," said Linda.

"I forgive you," replied the girl.

"The girl never asked me to forgive her," Linda told Susie, "but as far as I was concerned, a heavy burdened was lifted. The cord that held me back was cut; I released her and all the group of their debt and forgave them all through that one act."

Linda encouraged Susie to do the same with her hurts, encouraging her to be nice to everyone, to love them in spite of the hurts, and to release them of any debt they owed her. The Lord showed Susie that He was faithful and that He works all things for our good. Susie matured in many ways and continued to reach out to others with kindness. To be sure, God is very creative, and every situation is not going to turn out the same, but when Susie became a ninth grader, her classmates—many of whom had once ignored and even shunned her—voted her to be their ninth grade princess for homecoming. To Susie, this was confirmation to accept others regardless of whether they accepted her.

We are not responsible for other people's attitudes, only ours. If they do not forgive us, then the weight is on their shoulders. But for your children and you, not granting forgiveness is much like being connected to your past by a cord. As the years go by, you forget it is even there. You begin to add new relationships—even marriage and children. However, at some point, the cord that connects you to your past will become taut. It will bring you to an abrupt standstill because sooner or later unforgiveness will affect all other areas of your life. No longer will you be able to move forward in your relationship with God or anyone else for that matter.

A spirit of forgiveness is the only remedy for a spirit of bitterness and resentment. Forgiving someone else will require real humility, of course, but unless we teach our children to forgive others of their debts, we will never be able to teach them *acceptance*. Remember, among the Savior's final words on the cross were these: "Father, forgive them; for they do not know what they are doing" (Luke 23:34). We need to have the same humble attitude as Jesus (see Philippians 2:5–8).

It's important that as parents we lead the way when it comes to letting our children see the benefits of showing brotherly kindness through acceptance, availability, and accountability. Remember, when children are young, they learn the virtues by watching their parents as they relate with each other, with their children, and with people outside the home. That is particularly true when it comes to learning brotherly kindness.

We need to realize the incredible influence we have on their lives. On the next page we offer twelve "nuggets," valuable ways parents can model kindness to their children through their actions and attitudes, both to their children and others. Keep in mind that if we can help our children to add the virtue of brotherly kindness ("the love of brothers"—beloved, dear, friendly), they can be better equipped to influence others for Christ. (By the way, the list is only partial; you may add other "nuggets" as you read insightful Scriptures.)

Nuggets of Brotherly Kindness

Brotherly kindness is not contrived or pretentious but sincere. The more children can observe this virtue, the more they will understand that it is a powerful thing to accept and affirm others. Give them nuggets of brotherly kindness as they mature, even role-play them. Here are twelve golden nuggets your children can treasure as they see them in you and seek to imitate them.

1. Shake hands with people when you meet them.
2. Look them in the eyes.
3. Ask questions that have to do with their interests.
4. Be sensitive to outsiders; reach out and include people who are alone.
5. Do not put others down in order to build yourself up.
6. Instead of becoming jealous of others, learn from them.
7. Never slander a person.
8. Give others a chance; show them grace.
9. Do not judge too harshly, for we will be judged in the same way we judge others.
10. Avoid giving "looks" of disgust or annoyance.
11. Avoid negative body language (such as folding arms in front of chest, slouching in a seat).
12. Excuse yourself when you must leave a conversation abruptly.

THE SECOND COMPONENT:
AVAILABILITY

The second component of brotherly kindness may sound a little easier, but it's harder than you think. *Availability* means that you value the relationship enough to invest yourself in it. Jesus was available to thousands, but spent most of His time pouring His life into

His twelve disciples, and especially into three of them: Peter, James, and John.

We must stop here and say that if you are a stay-at-home mom (or dad) and work inside the home, do not think of your job as meaningless. Recognize that in your position of ongoing time with your children, you have the most important position in the world. The additional time to be available to your spouse and children can pay off in the present and the future.

If you work outside the home, you must pay close attention to the fact that your children will probably not receive instruction in these virtues in any day-care facility. Therefore, you will need to use your time wisely when you are with your family, practicing and nurturing these virtues in the hours you have with them.

If you are a father, remember that being available to your wife and children is a major priority, second only to your time alone with God. Just as Jesus was most available to Peter, James, and John, you need to be to your family. This will mean more to them than you can imagine, and God will richly bless the time that you invest with each of them.

In our third year of marriage, David and I both made a change in our careers. I stopped teaching home economics to be a stay-at-home mom, and David went from teaching English and coaching football and track to working as a financial advisor. We were both looking forward to our new careers.

Soon the summer and fall had passed, and our son John David was born. I loved being a mother, teaching Bible classes, and growing in my love for the Lord and my family. I remember saying, "Life doesn't get any better than this!" I could not have been happier and more content.

Three years later, however, I found myself sitting on my front porch feeling depressed and overwhelmed. I was reminded of the line from the Robert Frost poem: "Two roads diverged in a yellow wood, and I took the one less traveled by." The sharp contrast hit me hard; my life's story was reading more like, "Ten roads diverged in a yellow wood, and I took all ten!"

I was now the mother of two boys, teaching Bible classes, attending a weekly Bible study, working as an interior designer, mod-

eling, and teaching charm classes to teenage girls in a large department store. At the same time I was trying very hard to put the Lord
first, spend quality time with my family, and increase my physical
exercise and time with friends. As I sat on the porch, I literally count-
ed on my fingers all of my accomplishments and endeavors, but I
felt mixed emotions of pride, guilt, and overwhelming frustration.
Furthermore, I became disheartened with the realization that I had
been going the wrong way. As I was considering a time- or stress-
management class to alleviate such pandemonium, the Holy Spirit
began to speak to me as I recalled a Scripture I had previously studied: "You have perseverance and have endured for My name's sake,
and have not grown weary. But I have this against you, that you have
left your first love. Therefore remember from where you have fallen,
and repent and do the deeds you did at first" (Revelation 2:3–5).

Jesus had always been available to me; however, I frequently neglected to put Him first. It is easy to get caught up in the world's
value system, and like many people, I found myself among those
who "loved the approval of men rather than the approval of God"
(John 12:43). I felt as if I had to look a certain way, acquire more
possessions, and have a fulfilling career while also being a "super
mom" and wife. The words of Jesus to another busy woman came
to mind: "Martha, Martha, you are worried and bothered by so many
things; but only one thing is necessary, for Mary has chosen the good
part, which shall not be taken away from her" (Luke 10:41–42).

Through His Word, the Lord helped me to realize that only one
thing was necessary. I mentally dropped everything from my sched-
ule and purposed in my heart to keep Christ first and add back only
the "necessary things" as God made them clear. Apart from my Bible
study, I made myself fully *available* to my family (the necessary thing)
and to any other calling in which God lead me, which meant I had
to say no to many good things.

But how do you determine when to say yes? The Lord will show
you what has eternal value. For example, I had one more decorating
client to whom God led me. Her name was Sandra. After seven years
of periodically working with her, sharing Christ with her, and praying for her, she came to know the Lord Jesus Christ as her Messiah.

Had I not been available, I would have missed the opportunity to meet Sandra . . . now my lifelong friend.

Having a secular job does not mean that you cannot do your work to the Lord. But when that job comes between you and your "first love" and you are made to compromise your beliefs, it may be necessary to leave your job. Your life may be brimming full of activities, but unless the Lord has directed you to those things, you will not have contentment.

It has been eighteen years since my front-porch experience, and much of the fruit I see in my family is a result of the seeds that were planted that day. I learned that by being available to God first and my family second, He would reveal when and how I needed to be available to others.

THE THIRD COMPONENT:
ACCOUNTABILITY

Accountability is the third component of brotherly kindness. We all need someone who can encourage us to keep going when life is tough. We need someone who will challenge us to dig deeper in our walk with God. We also need someone we can share anything with and know it will be held in confidence. We need someone who will look out for our best interests and pray for us even when we do not ask for prayer. This someone is called an accountability partner.

An accountability partner can be valuable to your child's emotional and spiritual life. When a child is younger than ten years old, parents can act as their accountability partners, but when a child reaches about age ten, he could be encouraged to find a friend—a Christian friend—with whom he can partner. Preteens and teens can come together to pray for one another, memorize Scripture together, and simply share what is on their hearts.

Accountability partners are usually about the same age to enable them to relate on the same level. This is different from mentoring, when an older or more spiritually mature person is available to someone younger or less mature in his or her walk with God. However, older students or adults can make themselves available to younger students as their accountability partners. In fact, we as parents should be in prayer for godly mentors to come into the lives of our children or teens as God directs. Often they can reinforce what you have already been teaching.

Your child may find a like-minded, similar-age partner through his Sunday school class, neighborhood, or, if he attends a Christian school, in his class. Home-schooled children may have contact with other home schoolers their age through social activities and occasional joint classes; from here a home schooler may find a friend he'd want to know better and grow with spiritually.

WHAT ABOUT BOBBY?

Bobby grew up alone. His father, an alcoholic, physically and verbally abused Bobby's mother, brother, and him. His parents separated when he was in the seventh grade, and at that time Bobby started drinking heavily. He was only twelve years old.

For the next two years, he was nearly abandoned. His father did not care to see him, and his mother worked until very late at night. When she was not working, she was spending time with a male companion who did not care for Bobby either. This left him to prepare and eat his meals alone. Often he went without eating at all. Bobby was desperately seeking acceptance from someone who truly cared about him, but no one seemed to be available.

In the ninth grade, however, a classmate invited him on a weekend church retreat where he accepted Jesus Christ, and found that the church was filled with the brotherly kindness he had desired. Feeling accepted by the adults and students in the youth group, Bobby soon understood the love and availability that Christ had for him. After that he spent the majority of his time at the church leading discipleship groups, giving talks in front of the youth group, and being discipled by college students. Bobby spent most of his evenings "hanging out" at the church.

Now he is a junior in high school, and our son David is his discipleship group leader. He is constantly amazed and inspired by Bobby's spiritual maturity and consistency. Despite the lack of an encouraging home life, Bobby continues to pray for his parents' salvation. Most boys his age have pictures of athletes and musicians on their bedroom walls; Bobby has Bible verses all over his walls. (He uses a marker!) David says that Bobby is a spiritual forest fire set on revolutionizing his school (and the world) for Christ—simply because of the brotherly kindness of one classmate. When our children learn to be available to show kindness and compassion, they can influence the world around them.

THE RACE

The race run by Derek Redmond, the Olympic medal contender in the 1992 summer Olympic Games, demonstrated the power of kindness and compassion to influence lives. Officially, Derek's effort in the 400-meter semifinals was recorded as "race abandoned." But many who watched the race realized Derek was far from being abandoned. To the 65,000 fans in Barcelona, Spain, and the millions watching by television, his race was the epitome of Olympic perseverance —and of someone coming alongside to help.

The British runner ripped a hamstring muscle and fell to the track, still 250 meters from the finish line. His face contorted with pain, Derek got up and defiantly hobbled along the track.

Minutes passed and he was still struggling to finish the last 100 meters, when out of the top row of the stands, scaling a four-and-one-half-foot concrete wall, a man bolted onto the track. He put his arm around Derek for support. When Derek recognized his father, he burst into tears. Derek told him he had to finish the race.

"Well, we've started everything together. We'll finish this together," his father said. Using his dad as a human crutch, Derek and his father finished the race together.

Man's race is not the same as God's. We are inadequate to finish His race on our own; we need Him *and* each other. We need God's help, and it is because of His acceptance and availability that we can demonstrate brotherly kindness toward others. Paul wrote in Romans 12:10, "Be devoted to one another in brotherly love." And Jesus has called us brothers and sisters and friends! Think of it: Jesus, the Son of God, humbled Himself to your level so that you could be His friend and brother. If fact, as our "friend who sticks closer than a brother" (Proverbs 18:24), Jesus is the greatest accountability partner we can have. He listens, encourages, and motivates us to obey His word (John 14:23–24). Your child will certainly benefit in having a friend like Jesus so he can demonstrate brotherly kindness to others. He will also benefit by having another person as an accountability partner.

Because Jesus humbled Himself to become your friend and brother, should you not do the same for others? "Be devoted to one another in brotherly *love*," Paul wrote. Our next virtue will take us beyond brotherly *kindness* . . . to love. It is there that we will discover the most intimate of all virtues and look deeply into the heart of God.

F a n   t h e   F l a m e

1. Read Matthew 5:23–24; 6:14. Is there anyone in your life whom you are having trouble forgiving? (Did someone abuse you, ignore you, or cast insults at you? Were you overlooked for a promotion? Did someone steal from you or treat your friendship lightly?) Jesus understands your pain, but if you want true freedom, it is up to you, not the person who hurt you. Right now ask God to help you be the *strong one* and choose to *forgive and release* the person of his debt. Then ask God if you need to ask forgiveness from that person. What can doing this mean to your children?

2. How can you use Philippians 2:1–16 to encourage your child when he or she is having problems related to friendships?

3. Plan a time to share two great passages with your family: Romans 12:10–21 and 1 Peter 3:8–14. From the passages, together compile a list of the attributes.

4. As you think of your own spouse and children, identify at least one way that you can become more . . .

Accepting:

Available:

Accountable:

5. Because each virtue builds upon the others, the first five virtues will help your family and you in adding *brotherly kindness.* How do those five virtues, and in particular, self-control and perseverance, help us to focus more on others rather than ourselves?

The Big Question

How will brotherly kindness help your child know God better?

Family Activities

In the "Fan the Flame" questions for chapters 4 and 5, we looked at several Old Testament names of God. Here are two more powerful names of God to share with your family.

El Roi means "The God Who Sees." When Sarah drove her servant, Hagar, away (Genesis 16), Hagar learned something about God as she sat alone in the wilderness. Read this passage to your children and ask them what she learned.

Jehovah-jireh means "The Lord Will Provide." God revealed His name to Abraham when He provided a ram to sacrifice instead of Abraham sacrificing his son, Isaac (Genesis 22). Your child will be comforted to know that the ram was a foreshadowing of Jesus whom God would send to be our total provider and sustainer. Read the story with your children and help them see that God will provide for them in the area of friendships.

Ask your children to help you plan an activity in which you make yourselves available to help someone in need.

In addition, after you compile a list of the attributes under question three of "Fan the Flame," have the family add several to the list of "Nuggets for Brotherly Kindness." They could even be listed under categories: acceptance, availability, and accountability. Consider posting this list in a place where everyone in your family will see it and be reminded of this virtue.

Memory Verse

Have your children memorize Ephesians 4:32.

10

The Seventh Virtue: Love

And in your brotherly kindness, [add] love.
—2 PETER 1:7

It was 1946, and World War II was winding down. A young sailor, on final leave in Richmond, Virginia, headed for town to find some excitement. Sitting around a table in a bar and becoming frustrated with his surroundings, Johnny told his buddies that he was going for a walk. There had to be something better to hold his attention, he thought, as he stepped out of the bar onto the sidewalk—and suddenly there it was. For there just in front of him walked a beautiful, confident young woman with long dark hair. Getting in step, he said, "Going my way?"

His words seemed to fall on deaf ears as Sara tried to ignore him by turning to look in the jewelry store window. "Pick it out, and I'll buy it for you," Johnny said. Still ignoring this cocky young man in uniform, she walked on, never noticing that he was quite handsome. Insistent on meeting this girl, the sailor began to speak again when the girl interrupted him with a question quite out of the ordinary, "Sailor, are you a Christian?"

For a brief moment he thought back to earlier days, remembering a church experience in his hometown. During a revival at his church when he twelve, he felt God calling him for the first time, and he wanted to become a Christian—but no one told him how. And he knew that nothing had happened; nothing had changed. He thought that if he could be careful about his conduct and lifestyle, then maybe he could get "it," whatever "it" was.

Now he reflected on his navy days. He still hadn't answered the beautiful woman in front of him, but he had realized his moral values and standards were no longer sufficient to keep him strong. Just last Easter, his mother had even wrote him a letter explaining the meaning of the holiday. He knew his mother was a Christian and was praying for him.

About that time, God had spared his life in Chicago; the hotel in which he was supposed to stay caught on fire and took the lives of seventy-six people. His life was also spared when the ship he was suppose to be on was torpedoed and all but a few men died. Because of these events, realizing he had been spared repeatedly, he made resolutions to reform, quit all his bad habits, and get right with the Lord. He found these resolutions to be unsuccessful, however, since he still did not know Christ personally.

So now the once confident sailor faced with this question stood there and struggled for words. "Well . . . my parents are Christians. . . . My mother prays a lot." Afraid that she would have him down on his knees on the sidewalk, he said, "How would you like to go to a movie?" When he did not get the answer that he was looking for, he asked, "How would you like to get something to drink somewhere?"

"I don't think so," she responded.

"What *do* you do for fun?" he asked. "It seems like you're wasting your life."

Responding with a smile she said, "You don't know what a good life is until you accept the Lord Jesus. It isn't what you give up that will make you a Christian. It's receiving Christ that changes your life. You become a new person on the inside; and with this new nature, you enjoy the new things I have been talking to you about. You don't just give up bad habits and reform, but you actually receive a new nature."

Sara then handed him a gospel tract and said, "I'd encourage you to read this because it will explain what I have been telling you, and I'll be praying for you."

A GOSPEL TRACT, A QUESTION— AND BIG CHANGES

The young woman handed Johnny the tract, as she remembered the words of her mother. Sara was a student at Mary Washington College of the University of Virginia, and was on her way to the coal mining section of Virginia to teach vacation Bible school to children. Her mother had told her before she left, "There will be many servicemen in Richmond returning from the war. Here are some gospel tracts you can give them."

"May I write to you if I ever decide to become a Christian?" Johnny asked. Hesitating, she wrote her address on the back of the gospel tract. He carefully tucked it into his wallet and went back to tell his buddies that he was thinking about becoming a Christian. A close friend, upset and disturbed that he was about to blow their last liberty, said, "If you want to get religion, why not wait until you're out of the navy."

Calmly the young sailor replied, "Don't get upset; I have just met the woman I'm going to marry. I'm going for a drive to think about this, and I'll pick you up when I come back for the others." He spent that night sifting through his priorities and values and determined that when he returned home in four days, after his scheduled discharge from the navy, he would then become a Christian.

Soon he was back home on the farm, honorable discharge in hand and a seemingly bright future ahead. Late one night, though, Johnny began to ponder the words of the young, attractive college student. He tried hard to remember where he had put the tract, and then he recalled exactly where he had put it in his car. The young man began to read the tract; in fact, he read it three times.

Immediately, the plan of salvation was made very clear and concise, and in a short prayer, he confessed his sins and received Christ. It was settled, and he had no doubt about his conversion experience.

The next day he shared it with his mother and everyone else he could find. His mother could hardly believe it. She asked, "What brought this on?"

"While I was in Richmond, returning home from the navy, someone witnessed to me and gave me a gospel tract, and I've been thinking about it ever since."

His mother took him into her arms, and as she cried she said, "I've always prayed that if I couldn't lead you to Christ, that God would send someone else."

Immediately, a series of remarkable events followed. That same day he received a letter from a Christian university asking him to come. Then, within three days, Johnny was attending the Christian school and discovering what the "good life" was that the girl had described. Finally, during his first year at the school he realized that Christ was calling him into the ministry. He chose to heed the call.

Johnny decided to write and tell the girl who led him to the Lord about his experience. Had he waited a few days longer, he would not have had Sara's correct address, for she had given him her college address and was about to graduate.

"I'm the sailor in Richmond who wanted a date," he explained. "You would not give me a date, but you gave me the gospel. Now, not only am I a Christian, but God also called me into the ministry, and I need your prayers."

Sara wrote back. "Praise the Lord. I remember giving you the tract and I prayed for you that night, but I haven't thought about you since."

THE MEETING

After corresponding for six months, the sailor wanted to arrange a meeting over the Christmas holidays. Initially the young woman wrote that she would be unable to see him due to a family trip, but realizing the train would stop in his hometown for thirty minutes, she agreed to meet him there.

It was 12:30 at night, and the young woman and her parents stepped off the train to a very quiet and empty depot. Soon she saw a lone person off in the distance at the other end of the station, and her parents suggested that she begin walking in that direction. As they approached one another, he asked, "Hello. Are you Sara?"

"Yes. Are you Johnny?" So Sara's father bought them a cup of coffee. It was the first time to see each other since their meeting in Richmond, and Johnny was excited to share about his plans for the ministry.

Soon, Sara and Johnny fell in love, and they were married three years later.

GENUINE, SACRIFICIAL LOVE

This is a story of love—one person loving Christ, loving the body of Christ, and loving the lost world enough to make Him known. This kind of love comes only from God. It is not a sexual love *(eros),* or even a friendship love *(philos)* but a sacrificial love given by God in order that the world might know God and His Son Jesus Christ. The Greek word for God's love is *agape,* meaning "love and goodwill." The verb tense is *agapao,* meaning "to love—sacrificially and unconditionally." Sara made several sacrifices to tell Johnny of God's love. She presented the gospel and then gave him a tract, not knowing whether he would reject the message or even ridicule her. She let him write her, showing sensitivity and compassion (although she did not give her home address). She took time to pray for him. "God is love" (1 John 4:8), and without knowing Him we cannot know genuine love.

After Sara and Johnny married, they would rear four daughters —I was one of them. It is this same kind of love that kept me persevering (sometimes all night) to rear, with my husband, three children of our own—and to write these pages.

Throughout the ages, men and women, boys and girls have worn Christian pins, bracelets, and rings, and put crosses on chains and fish symbols on their cars, hoping to catch the attention of a nonbelieving world. But, for the most part, the world has not been impressed. Crosses are often worn by blasphemous heathens; blatant atheists have added feet to our fish symbol—rejecting creation; and we are surrounded by a world that has little or no regard for absolute truth. The world has turned its back and has chosen rather to call us hypocrites.

Of course, there is nothing wrong with Christian symbols, but there is a better sign that Jesus said would catch the onlooker's attention and stand the test of time until His return.

Just hours before His arrest, Jesus, in anticipation of His death, gave His disciples the final apologetic—the seventh virtue. "A new commandment I give to you, that you love one another, even as I have loved you," He said during the Last Supper with them. "By this all men will know that you are My disciples, if you have love for one another" (John 13:34–35).

To love like Jesus loved is the mark we teach our children to wear so they might show that God sent Jesus and that we are His disciples. This is what would get the attention of the world. Francis A. Schaeffer calls it *the mark of the Christian,* and the final apologetic that the world needs in order to believe.

But maybe you are asking yourself, "What's the connection between Jesus departing from earth and giving His disciples a new commandment to *love one another?* Would they not be able to love one another without Him?"

Peter had told Jesus, "I will lay down my life for You" (John 13:37). Before Peter realized it, he had denied Jesus three times, even cursing when he did. He had failed Jesus miserably. Later, after Jesus had been crucified and was resurrected, He appeared to some of His disciples and asked Peter three thought provoking questions:

"Simon [Peter] . . . do you love Me more than these?"; "Simon . . . do you love Me?"; and "Simon . . . do you love Me?" (John 21:15–17).

Maybe Jesus wanted to give Peter a chance to make up for the three times he had denied Him, but we want you to see something a little deeper. The first two times that Jesus asks Peter if he loved Him, the word He used in Greek was *agapao.* This Greek verb means "to love—sacrificially and unconditionally." All three times Peter responded, "You know that I love You," and all three times the Greek rendering for the love he used was *phileo,* which you are already familiar with from our last chapter. It means "to love with a brotherly love."

However, when Jesus asked the questions, only the third time did He use Peter's terminology, saying *"phileo."* The first two times, Jesus had asked whether Peter had a sacrificial agape love. No wonder Peter was grieved when Jesus asked him the third time. Jesus was offering Peter His shepherding job, and the only requirement Peter needed on his resume was "I love *(agapao)* Jesus," but Peter was unable to love *(agapao)* the way Jesus could. There was Jesus right in front of him. As much as Peter wanted to love Jesus and as much as he had experienced the love of Jesus and wanted to emulate Him, he could not love to the same extent Jesus could. He could not love his Messiah and others this way until Jesus ascended and sent His Holy Spirit to live in Peter.

When the Holy Spirit came upon Peter and the others who were waiting, Scripture indicates they were filled with power! Immediately the Holy Spirit supplied Peter with the unconditional love and bold truth of God that the disciple would need to preach one of the most dynamic sermons ever preached; three thousand souls were added that day (see Acts 24:4, 14–41). Now he understood what Jesus meant when He said, "Feed My sheep."

Peter later wrote, "Since you have in obedience to the truth purified your souls for a sincere love *[phileo]* of the brethren, fervently love *[agapao]* one another from the heart" (1 Peter 1:22). Brotherly kindness had prepared them for brotherly love. The first kind of love, *phileo,* comes from a pure soul (mind, will, emotions); the second, *agapao,* comes from a pure heart (the inner spirit controlled by the Holy Spirit). With the Holy Spirit's help, Peter was now able to say, "I love You, Jesus" and be obedient to His command. God's love not only changes us, but it also changes others through us.

This seventh virtue, love, is what makes us complete in Christ. Remember, it was Peter who penned for us the seven virtues through the inspiration of the Holy Spirit. We cannot fully know Christ without practicing *all* seven virtues. Peter's life dramatically changed once he received the Holy Spirit and began practicing these virtues. Peter had himself stumbled very badly by denying that he knew Jesus, so is it any wonder that he lovingly reminds us that if we practice these virtues, we will "never stumble." Jesus even wanted to make sure that we might be able to "call them to mind" after He was gone.

HELPING OUR CHILDREN
DEVELOP LOVE . . . BY LOVING

As parents, we cannot force our children to wear the mark; it must come from a willing heart inspired by the Holy Spirit. However, we can still explain and demonstrate *love* while spending time with our children as Jesus did in teaching His disciples before they were filled with the Holy Spirit. Once your child has accepted Christ person-ally, the Holy Spirit will guide him into all truth. *Then* when you teach him something concerning love, the Spirit will bear witness to him what he should do; your child should begin to increase in his ability to show agape love.

So now we are faced with the question, "How *did* Jesus love?" The apostle John wrote, "We know love by this, that He laid down His life for us; and we ought to lay down our lives for the brethren. . . . Little children, let us not love with word or with tongue, but in deed and truth" (1 John 3:16, 18). Such love carries a double emphasis, for Jesus commanded us to love our neighbors as ourselves (see Matthew 22:39).

But how do we teach our children to love the way He did? This is not easy. Even those who are mature, adult Christians have diffi-culty loving others in the way Jesus commands, "to lay down our lives" (though in many cases people in other countries are dying on behalf of others). A good explanation to give our children for this command is, "to give up what we might want for the benefit of some-one else."

We should not be surprised if our children do not consistently demonstrate this virtue of agape love. They may try to please you and do the things that you say exhibit love, but unless the Spirit of God lives in them as believers, they will never truly understand the value of "love." Even when they do receive Christ, you must be pa-tient with them as they learn to give up their rights on behalf of others. That, of course, will be a challenge. That is why we as parents need to become conscious of modeling agape love. The more our children see love in action, the more natural it will be for them to do the same.

This begins with truly loving our children—not giving up our-selves so that they can have everything they want but consistently showing unconditional love towards them regardless of circumstances or punishments. Being loved unconditionally by someone else helps us to understand the God who created us and died for us and will glorify us in the day of resurrection.

As your children learn to love God and have a passion for Him, they discover that they cannot keep Him to themselves. God's Spirit within them will want to testify of Jesus. When this happens, they will begin to understand the meaning of having true "knowledge of the Lord Jesus Christ" (2 Peter 1:8).

THE DUAL MISSION OF LOVE

To explain what we mean, take a look at Jesus' twofold mission, found in His prayer and message in John 17: "O righteous Father, although the world has not known You, yet I have known You; and these have known that You sent Me; and I have made Your name known to them, and will make it known, so that the love with which You loved Me may be in them, and I in them" (verses 25–26).

Jesus has described the message of love in a nutshell. Do you see it? Look again. How did the disciples know that God had sent Jesus? What two things convinced them?

The reason that Jesus was able to say to His Father that He had "accomplished the work" was that *they knew*. And He did it in two ways: "I have known You . . . and I have made Your name known."

As much as we try to make Christianity difficult, it is really *this* simple: To know Him and to make Him known. This is what gives our life purpose and meaning. This is how we can know God's will. This is how we feel real "accomplishment." The more you know Him, the more you will love Him, and the more you love Him, the more you will love others enough to make Him known.

This is the work to which God calls us. It begins with our children displaying a love that they have seen as good and admirable in us and with learning about a Savior whom, through the Holy Spirit's prompting, they may desire.

HELPING OUR CHILDREN KNOW HIM BETTER

Knowing God and His love for us helps us to love one another, including our children, and this exalts His name on the earth. We cannot know everything there is to know about God, but we can know more about Him. The more one wants to know God, the more God will reveal Himself to the person. This takes work. Most of us are too busy to know Him, but if we make it a priority in our own lives to get to know Him, eventually our children will have the desire to know Him as well. This will result ultimately in their making Him known.

Eugene Peterson, writer of *The Message* translation of the New Testament, said, "Busyness is laziness." Jesus spent an incredible amount of time seeking the Father in prayer and yet had time for others. In fact, that is why He spent the time to know the Father.

For our children, knowing God will be a growth process. During His childhood years, even Jesus "kept increasing in wisdom and stature, and in favor with God and men" (Luke 2:52). How do our children get to know God? By helping your child add these seven virtues to their faith, you will be helping them to *know God*. This will send them on their way to *making Him known*. As we noted, these virtues find their fullest expression when our children have received a new life in Christ (see 2 Corinthians 5:17). When they do not know the Savior personally, they cannot regularly display the virtues, for the Holy Spirit is not within them.

That raises the question, How can children know more about Jesus? Here are three ways you can help your children gain a fuller understanding of who Jesus is:

1. Remind your children of the sacrifice that Jesus made for them. (He loved them enough to die for them.) Tell them the story of His passion—the events of His submission and death—every so often, not just on Good Friday or Easter Sunday. They can be introduced to His sacrificial love while they are young. I remember taking our children when they were babies to the church nursery, and their teacher would take them in her arms and hold them close and say, "Jesus loves you and so do I." She taught me that children are never too young to learn about God's love.
2. Encourage daily Bible reading. "Whoever keeps His word, in him the love of God has truly been perfected" (1 John 2:5). God's Word helps us to know Him better. The more we know Him, the more we love Him. The more we love Him, the more we will make Him known. An amazing thing happens in the

process of knowing Him: others catch a glimpse of His eternal love—by no means of our own effort except that of keeping His Word.

3. Encourage them to pray. Praying is the most intimate thing we can do with God. Jesus loved God; He loved His Word enough to keep it and teach it. He also knew the value of being alone in prayer with God, and as He did, He understood His Father's will. And our children can learn to take time to pray as well. Even if your children do not have a personal relationship with Christ, they may pray with you and their prayers be carried to God through your praying on their behalf at the same time. And God does at times hear the pleas of the unsaved as they seek His face.

MAKING HIM KNOWN

If (or when) your child has received Jesus as his Savior from personal sin, he will express that love more fully. Such love will include telling friends about Jesus' love for them. Do not underestimate a child's capability in making Jesus known. However, in sharing his or her faith, it will help your child to see a role model; hopefully that role model can be you.

My grandmother, Nana, lived her life to witness for Jesus. I (Anne) remember driving up to a gas station as a teenager with my grandmother in the car. She kept a purse full of gospel tracts (she passed that habit to Sara, who gave a tract to my future father during their first meeting) and she would hand me one and say, "Here, give this to the attendant." Still a little timid I would say, "Here, my grandmother wants me to give this to you." It would be years before I too became bold in sharing the gospel. In the months before she died, she would call from her bed, "Come on King Jesus." She would also invite people to her own funeral! For, you see, death to her meant life.

When the Holy Spirit is in control of our lives, our witnessing becomes spontaneous; it is almost effortless; that is His purpose. Jesus said of the Holy Spirit: "When the Helper comes, whom I will send to you from the Father, that is the Spirit of truth who proceeds from the Father, He will testify about Me" (John 15:26). That is good news.

As Oswald Chambers noted:

> The love of God is only in us when it has been shed abroad in our hearts by the Holy Spirit, and the evidence that it is there is the spontaneous way in which it is manifested.
>
> No love on earth will develop without being cultivated. We have to dedicate ourselves to love, which means identifying ourselves with God's interests in other people, and God is interested in some funny people, viz., in you and in me!…God's love for me is inexhaustible, and His love for me is the basis of My love for others."[1]

As a parent, your consistent acts of love will impress your children; they will watch the impact of love. I remember my father's example. Since he was a pastor and our name was "Adkerson," he was usually the first "Rev." that troubled street people saw in the phone book, the first minister whom they called. I remember going with him to take food to a drunken destitute who lived in the *bad part of town*. I remember seeing my mother putting together food and clothing to give a woman who came begging at our door.

Over the years it was exciting to see people come to know the Lord and in turn watch them share their faith with others who also received Christ. There is nothing more thrilling than when God uses us to draw others to Himself.

SHOWING HIS LOVE

Showing His love in natural ways is the key in presenting an attractive Savior and winning the respect and attention of a world of dying people. True agape love should occur in our children regularly when they have Jesus leading their lives. But even if our children don't have a relationship, they can on occasion show love as they watch us. As parents and Christians, we will often have several marks of love that our children will see and imitate.

Here are ten observable deeds that mark a Christian: (1) combine truth with grace; (2) serve one another; (3) deny your desires for the sake of others; (4) find common ground with people who are different; (5) handle your differences differently than the nonbeliever does; (6) regard others as more important; (7) be ready to tell others about Christ; (8) love without fear; (9) watch for answered prayer; and (10) be joyful.

Those marks of Christian love are described in the accompanying list on pages 190–92. We want to highlight two.

First, tell others about Christ (number seven). Teach your children about Andrew who brought his brother Simon (Peter) to Jesus (John 1:40). Help your children find answers to their questions so that they can give answers to others. It is not how much they know but *who* they know. "Now as they observed the confidence of Peter and John and understood that they were uneducated and untrained men, they were amazed, and began to recognize them as having been with Jesus" (Acts 4:13).

Second, live without fear (number eight). We often become fearful that our children cannot be trusted, or that they will be taken advantage of, or that they will not be successful. We are sometimes fearful that our children will not love us if we discipline them, and the list goes on.

When you submit your fears to Christ, you feel God's peace (Philippians 4:6–7), and your children sense that peace and are reassured. In addition, they learn through prayer and trust to give their fears to God.

Our children can live with the same kinds of fears, but fear is not from God. It is the work of Satan. Help your children learn to trust God. It may take time, but when they do they will be a testimony to the world (Psalm 4:8; 56:4; 91; Isaiah 41:10; Matthew 6:25–34).

Ten Observable Deeds That Mark a Christian:

1. Combine truth with grace (John 1:17). There will be times when a situation comes up with your child that requires confrontation. This is an opportunity to communicate the truth in love. As you describe the situation while under control, always looking out for the child's interests, you confront, clarify, and correct. Your child will see—and later he may imitate—this powerful way of love in his relationships.

2. Serve one another (Hebrews 12:28). Teach your children to do for others expecting nothing in return. Our children can learn servanthood in many ways: helping someone else with his chores, picking up sticks or mowing the grass for an elderly person without charge, and volunteering for community service. During Thanksgiving, for instance, you and your children can help serve food to the needy at a local shelter or the Salvation Army.

3. Deny self on behalf of others (Luke 9:23; Romans 14–15; 1 Peter 3:16–17). Children need to learn that sometimes they must deny themselves of something they might consider good, if it could cause their Christian brother to stumble.

4. Find common ground with people who are different (1 Corinthians 9:22). We must show our children by example the importance of finding common ground with those who are different than we are. Children can learn to look past differences in personalities, looks, backgrounds, and cultures to find common ground. And we should remind our children that others do not need to agree with them to make them feel accepted. Our children simply need to understand that acceptance paves the way to influence.

5. Handle your differences differently than the world; always work toward resolution rather than trying to win. It is normal to disagree, but the world will sit up and take notice when we humble ourselves at all costs to settle the issues. Remember it is not always the wrong one but the strong one who should attempt to restore a broken relationship. If your child has an argument with a friend, he must first learn to have regret over the broken relationship. Then he must work toward resolution

by asking forgiveness for his part and being willing to offer forgiveness if his friend asks. If his friend is not willing to forgive him, at least he has planted seeds of love as an example to his friend. When restitution is made, this will show *their* world that they can still love each other (Ephesians 5:1–21; 1 Corinthians 13). Don't return evil for evil; give a blessing instead (1 Peter 3:9; Romans 13:10; 1 Thessalonians 4:1–12).

6. Regard others as more important than yourself (Philippians 2:3–10). Teach your children to be interested in others by asking questions about them and not just talking about themselves. Teach them to offer up the best toy, snack, or seat to others before choosing. Tell them that God will bless them because they will be acting as Christ did—Christ became like a servant, but God exalted Him. Make sure you praise them when you see them demonstrating love.

7. Be ready to tell others about Christ (1 Peter 3:15). There is a world out there dying for answers. The apostle Peter wrote that we should be ready to answer "everyone who asks [us] to give an account for the hope that is in [us]" (1 Peter 3:15). Children can give great answers or at least find someone who can. Your child's loving action in sharing the good news of Jesus can have a lasting impact. In chapter 4 we mentioned how David led his friend Ben to the Lord after a fraternity party. Ben is now one of the youth leaders in the church near his college campus. He disciples his own group of boys and has invested his life in multitudes of people at church, school, and work by sharing his faith and simply loving them for Christ's sake.

8. Live without fear (1 John 4:18). Why should the world trust in our God if they see us living in fear? We are fearful that God cannot be trusted so we take things into our own hands. We fear if we do not have a quick answer from God. We fear that someone might get ahead of us spiritually, financially, occupationally. We fear losing the people and things we love and being alone. We can be afraid of not having enough food or eating too much food. We fear our children may become sick or contract a dangerous disease; they may not be accepted or loved by their peers. But such fear need not rule over us. According

to 1 John 4:18, "Perfect love casts out fear, because fear involves punishment, and the one who fears is not perfected
in love."

9. Answered prayers (John 15:7–10). Pray about everything! Remind your children that nothing is too big or too small to
pray about. An answered prayer can encourage others to pray
and can be an easy testimony to share with others. People
throughout history have been inspired to worship God because of answered prayers. (The book of Daniel is representative of this.)

10. Joy (1 Peter 1:8). It is natural to want to be around joyful people. Joy only comes from the Lord; the more our children
know God, the more joyful they will become. As parents,
we need to be mindful that too often we stifle their joy by the
cares of the world. In truth, we are most joyful when we are
content with godliness and not what the world has to offer.
You may want to tell your children about Paul and Silas, who
had joy while in jail (Acts 16:14–34). Remember that joy
comes from "the God of hope [who fills] you with all joy
and peace in believing, so that you will abound in hope by
the power of the Holy Spirit" (Romans 15:13).

In addition to teaching your children the way of love and demonstrating your love as a useful servant of God, look for opportunities
to share the good news of Jesus. Witnessing should be part of a normal lifestyle. There may be opportunities with everyday contacts,
and your children will look over your shoulder. Our children grew
up hearing us tell others about God's love. Those instances involved
sharing with baby-sitters, a lifeguard, business associates, friends at
birthday parties, strangers in stores, car wash attendants, and the list
goes on.

But what is really exciting is when our children make Him
known. One day while praying with my Moms In Touch group, I
offered up only one prayer—that our children would be witnesses
at school. That afternoon our son Daniel walked in the door, and

the first thing he said was, "I witnessed to someone today." He was in the fifth grade, and I was so thrilled. I said, "Daniel, that's great. Tell me about it."

He said, "Well, I was talking to my friend Leo, and I said, 'Leo, are you a Christian?' And Leo said, 'No.' So I said, 'Well, would you like to be?' And he said, 'Yes.' So I told him, 'All you have to do is ask Jesus to come into your heart.' So Leo bowed his head to pray. Then I interrupted him and said, 'Oh yeah, first of all you have to ask Him to forgive you of your sins.' So he bowed his head to pray again." And Leo experienced the love of God.

Francis Schaeffer says, "The word *love* should not be just a banner. In other words, we must do whatever must be done, at whatever the cost, to show this love. So often people think that Christianity is only soft, only a kind of gooey love that loves evil equally with good. This is not the Biblical position. The holiness of God is to be exhibited simultaneously with love."[2]

PUTTING IT ALL TOGETHER

Loving others is easier when we ask Jesus to love others through us. However, it is not easy to come to the point of asking Him. First, we must learn to respect and obey God's authority—goodness. Second, we must spend time meditating on God's Word—knowledge. Third, we must practice allowing the Spirit to have control over our flesh—self-control. Fourth, we must come to the point where we trust God in *all* of our circumstances—perseverance. Fifth, we must come to realize that *He* is our life, and *everything* we do, we do to please Him—godliness. Sixth, we must learn to reach out with kindness and overcome evil with good—brotherly kindness.

With such virtues in practice, the knowledge that we gain of God and His Son, Jesus, enables us to cultivate a passion for God and a love for His children. This is it; this is love. It is first and foremost on God's heart, and when we obey His commandment to love one another, we demonstrate that we love Him and know Him (see 1 John 2:5; 4:7–8; 5:3).

It all begins with faith in Jesus Christ. It will be *your* victory, your *child's* victory, your *church's* victory, and the *world's* victory. As the apostle John wrote, "For whatever is born of God overcomes the world; and this is the victory that has overcome the world—our faith" (1 John 5: 4).

Imagine for a moment what it would be like if every believer truly practiced these seven virtues—if we loved others as perfectly as we wanted to be loved. Imagine the relationship you would have with your spouse. Imagine the unity your family would have.

Let us practice these virtues. When we do, we will benefit our children and honor our Father in heaven.

Our prayer for you and your children echoes that of the apostle Paul:

> *That [the Father] would grant you, according to the riches of*
> *His glory, to be strengthened with power through His Spirit*
> *in the inner man, so that Christ may dwell in your hearts*
> *through faith; and that you, being rooted and grounded in*
> *love, may be able to comprehend with all the saints*
> *what is the breadth and length and height and depth,*
> *and to know the love of Christ which surpasses knowledge,*
> *that you may be filled up to all the fullness of God.*
>
> EPHESIANS 3:16–19

Fan the Flame

1. Read Colossians 2:1–10. List at least seven results or benefits that Paul gives of "having been knit together in love" (verse 2). What can these mean for your children?

2. What is the true test that "the love of God has truly been perfected" in our children and in us (1 John 2:5)?

3. What does 1 John 3:18 say about love? What are three ways you can help your children practice the truth of this verse? (Refer to the list within this chapter of the ten suggestions that mark a Christian.)

4. Read Philippians 1:6–11, 27. What is Paul's message to the Philippians, and what is the heart of his prayer for them? What personal message do you gain from this passage? We encourage you to use Paul's prayer in verses 9–11 as a prayer for your children.

5. Complete your study by reading again 2 Peter 1:1–15. In light of all you have read and practiced, what value is there for increasing in these seven virtues?

The Big Question

How does practicing love help your child know God better?

Family Activities

During your family time, read and discuss Luke 10:30–37. When you get to verse 36, ask them the question that Jesus asked. On a different night, read and discuss verses 38–42 with your family. Ask each child to describe the "one" most important thing in life. Then ask your children to describe the things that are necessary in their lives. Help them to begin prioritizing their little worlds. Ask them if they are worried and bothered about anything. Use this time as an opportunity to pray for one another's needs so that you can all focus on what truly counts.

Spend time this week praying with your children that they would not only feel God's love for them but would want to show His *agape* love to others. Then tell them you will begin to pray for them the prayers of love and wisdom found in the New Testament. Each week pray one of the following prayers on their behalf, remembering that when we use Scripture, we are praying according to God's will: Ephesians 1: 16–20; 3: 14–20; Philippians 1: 9–11; Colossians 1: 9–12.

For a special activity, plan getaways with your family several times a year. Go to the mountains for an overnight trip and hike, collect leaves, pan for gems, have a picnic, etc. Go to the beach or a rodeo or circus or fair. (Wherever you go, make sure the location is far enough to be out of town, but not so far that you become tired or frustrated in driving.) The main goal is to try to get away for a couple of days—away from everyday activities where the family can relax, talk, and simply be together in a fun environment. Regardless of what happens while you are away, you will have made a memory.

Memory Verse

Have your children memorize 1 John 3:18.

Notes

Chapter 2: Fan the Flame with Positive Words

1. Ron Willingham, *When Good Isn't Good Enough* (New York: Doubleday, 1989), 4–5.
2. Ibid., 6.

Chapter 3: Spark an Interest in Knowing God

1. James Mallory, Conference on Integration of Spiritual and Psychological Factors and Mental Health, Palm Beach, Florida, 7 February 1999.

Chapter 4: The First Virtue: Goodness

1. All Greek (and Hebrew) translations in this chapter are taken from Robert L. Thomas, ed., *The New American Exhaustive Concordance of the Bible* (Nashville: Holman, 1981).

Chapter 5: The Second Virtue: Knowledge

1. John F. Walvoord and Roy B. Zuck, *The Bible Knowledge Commentary: The New Testament* (Wheaton, Ill.: Victor, 1983), 865.
2. As quoted in Michael P. Green, ed., *Illustrations for Biblical Preaching* (Grand Rapids: Baker, 1989), 18.

Chapter 7: The Fourth Virtue: Perseverance

1. As quoted by Janet Parshall, "What's for Sale in the Marketplace of Ideas?" Rebuilding the Walls Seniors Conference, Focus on the Family, Colorado Springs; audio tape message on 10 September 1999 (1-888-228-2737).

2. Andrew Jukes, *The Names of God* (Grand Rapids, Mich.: Kregel, 1976), 74–79; as quoted in Kay Arthur, *Lord I Want to Know You* (Sisters, Ore.: Multnomah, 1992), 46–47.

Chapter 8: The Fifth Virtue: Godliness

1. Dan DeHaan, *The God You Can Know* (Chicago: Moody, 1982), 84.

2. C. S. Lewis, *The Screwtape Letters,* in *The Best of C. S. Lewis* (New York: Macmillan, 1977), 39–40.

3. Ibid., 51–52.

Chapter 9: The Sixth Virtue: Brotherly Kindness

1. Raghu Rai and Navin Chawla, *Faith and Compassion: The Life and Work of Mother Teresa* (Rockport, Maine: Element Books, 1996), 191–92.

Chapter 10: The Seventh Virtue: Love

1. As quoted in *Our Brilliant Heritage* (Fort Washington, Pa.: Christian Literature Crusade, 1929), 117.

2. Francis Schaeffer, *The Mark of the Christian* (Downers Grove, Ill.: InterVarsity, n. d.), 28.

Resource One
Grandparents in Action

*A*lthough parents play the primary role in lighting a child's passion for God, grandparents can help. Here are specific ways grandparents can focus their grandchildren on God through acts of lovingkindness.

First, encourage them. An easy and personal way to encourage your grandchildren is by writing them letters. Fill the mailbox every couple of months with letters to "Master Steven" or "Miss Susan." Send funny and colorful cards on any occasions not just on their birthdays. Children love to get mail. And of course, encourage them with phone calls.

Letters can inspire, comfort, and even teach your grandchildren. We remember one letter that David's dad wrote our sons years ago at the end of a little league football season:

Dear Daniel and David,
>   Congratulations! You are true champions!
>   As you look back over the season you can recall many times of hard

work, sweat, and pain, as well as the pleasure of success. There are several very important lessons you have learned; hard work, dedication, determination, and success are not just words—you have felt them and know what they are like.

These same lessons can be applied to all phases of life! So keep it up! We are all so very proud of you, not just for being champions but for making the effort, for staying with what you started, for making good grades, and studying even when you didn't feel like it.

You have grown in many ways. Football is merely a game; what you've accomplished is more than a game. Keep striving and do your best! You have the best role model a boy could ever have—your dad!

With much love and devotion,
Pappa John

In your letters and phone calls, look for different ways to affirm your grandchildren. It means so much to parents when grandparents not only encourage their grandchildren personally but also affirm them in listening to their parents Besides writing letters, there are other ways in which you can encourage your grandchildren.

- Send occasional packages with goodies reflecting their favorite hobby when the child has accomplished a certain goal (Scripture memory, good grades, different acts of kindness, etc.).
- Attend school events, music performances, athletic events, plays, etc. that you are aware of. A child feels extra special when he knows that his grandparents care enough to support his interests.
- Start a college fund for the child, which you add to every year. It may not mean much to him or her as a youngster, but it will be greatly appreciated later.
- Help your grandchild build a tree house, or hang a rope swing in your yard for your grandchildren to play on when visiting you.
- Allow your grandchildren to bake cookies, cupcakes, biscuits, etc., when they visit you. When David's mother died from cancer, we requested the old ceramic bowl that she and Lauren would make biscuits in. Lauren has wonderful memories of standing on a chair as she sifted, stirred, kneaded, and cut mouth-

watering biscuits. Daniel will never forget making a delicious batch of chocolate chip cookies with my mother.

Second, pray for them. We believe grandparents are especially good at this. My mother has a daily prayer list, and on her list she has the names of all her children and ten grandchildren. About ten years ago, she was diagnosed with multiple sclerosis, which slowed her down in many ways, but it did not slow her prayer life. She has remained in continual prayer through the years, praying throughout the day as the Spirit of God leads her. I am sure she often prays for things that I am not able to sense the need to pray for myself.

Our children are well aware of the fact that she prays diligently for them daily. One day, our son Daniel said, "Mom, if anything ever happens to Mamma Sara, you are just going to have to drop everything and just pray." She has truly taught our children the value of prayer.

There were many times that one of our nieces would call her grandmother even in the wee hours of the morning anxiously concerned about something. She would not have awakened her own parents but felt completely confident that her grandmother would be happy to talk to her—and her grandmother was and even encouraged it.

Third, teach them God's Word. We don't mean just read Scripture to them; have them read Scripture, or help them in Bible memory work. Be creative, helping them love to learn the Word and the principles for life that it teaches.

Our dear friends Mal and Wanda McSwain, in ministry with Young Life, have two children also involved in Christian ministry. Knowing that their children are fully capable of teaching spiritual truths to their grandchildren does not inhibit them from participating in the fun. Grandparents often have more time to plan and discover creative ways of teaching about God than parents do. For instance, not long ago Wanda invited her grandchildren, ages three to ten, for a four-day adventure at her home, which she called "God's Beautiful World Club." As they arrived, Wanda greeted them with safari hats that she had crafted by tying animal print fabric around various straw hats. She even set up a tent to be their home base. Each day the children would take a nature walk and inspect plants, animals, birds, insects, and rocks, as Wanda presented related stories from the Bible on God's creation. The children all left with a portfolio of collages, specimens, and pictures representing God's incredible power, beauty, and imagination.

You do not have to be creative in order to teach your grandchildren the Word of God in a positive way. Here are other simple yet personal ways you can teach them:

- Have a colorful Bible storybook on hand to read at bedtime.
- Share with your grandchildren things that God is teaching you. This will demonstrate to them that God continues to teach us over the course of our lives.
- Sit down and have a snack with your grandchild and simply ask questions such as, "What do you think God is like?" or, "Who do you think made the raisins that are in these cookies?" Before you know it, your grandchild will be asking you questions, but do not feel like you have to have all the answers. It is fine for him to ponder his unanswered questions.

Resource Two

Training Our Children with Scripture

*T*he training of our children will be only as effective as the truth we teach and demonstrate. Our children are making mental notes to see if our words and actions line up with what we are trying to teach them before they accept it as truth. It is of great importance to us to refresh our memories about what the Bible has to say about truth.

Before you consider a Scripture memorization time for your children, be convinced personally of its benefits, and be able to answer your children's common question, "Why?" The answer is found in the Bible verses that follow.

TRAINING OUR CHILDREN ABOUT THE TRUTHS IN SCRIPTURE

Beside each passage, write down key thoughts you want to remember to teach your children about God's Word and about truth, which is recorded in God's Word.

3 John 1:3–4 (also Galatians 4:19) _____

_____

1 John 1:6 _____

_____

2 Timothy 2:15 _____

_____

2 Timothy 4:2–4 _____

_____

Ephesians 4:15 _____

_____

John 3:21 _____

_____

John 8:32 _____

_____

John 17:17 _____

_____

John 16:7–14 _____

_____

Luke 20:21 _____

_____

MEMORY VERSES FOR
YOUNGER AND OLDER CHILDREN

Here are a list of verses about the gospel, the nature of God, and the power of Scriptures that are suitable for both young and older children.

John 3:16	Proverbs 3:3	Philippians 4:19
Romans 8:28	2 Corinthians 5:17	1 Corinthians 10:13
1 John 4:19	Matthew 6:33	James 1:19–20
2 Timothy 2:15	1 Timothy 4:12	Ephesians 4:32
2 Timothy 3:16	Proverbs 3:5–6	Philippians 4:11
1 John 4:7	1 Peter 5:6	2 Thessalonians 3:3
1 Corinthians 15:33	Psalm 139:14	Philippians 2:13
2 Timothy 1:7	Jeremiah 33:3	Philippians 2:3
Psalm 34:1	1 John 1:9	Ephesians 6:1–3
Romans 1:16	Romans 12:1–2	

VERSES FOR CHILDREN
TO SHARE THE GOSPEL

Romans 3:23	Romans 5:8	1 John 1:9
Romans 6:23	Ephesians 2:8–9	John 3:16
Revelation 3:20	1 John 5:11–13	Romans 10:9–10
John 14:6		

OTHER PASSAGES TO MEMORIZE

1 Corinthians 10:15	2 Peter 3:9–15	Jeremiah 29:11–13
Galatians 6:7–9	1 Thessalonians 4:3–7	1 John 2:15–17
2 Corinthians 10:3–6	1 Peter 3:15	Ephesians 4:29–32
2 Corinthians 10:12	2 Chronicles 16:9	Philippians 1:6
Romans 6:10–14	Jeremiah 9:23–24	Philippians 1:21
Psalm 19	Isaiah 30:21	Psalm 100
Philippians 2:10–15	1 Corinthians 9:24–27	Psalm 23
Ephesians 6:10–18	1 Peter 5:6–10	Psalm 1
Galatians 5:16	1 Timothy 4:7b–8	Joshua 1:8–9
Galatians 5:22–23	1 Timothy 6:6–11	

Resource Three
Learning Self-Control

LEARNING SELF-CONTROL ...
THROUGH STUDYING THE SCRIPTURES

Scripture can help your children build self-control by strengthening their inner spirit. Here are verses that will give your children strength for resisting temptation. They may reflect on these Scriptures before the temptation comes, and may choose to memorize those that are particularly helpful. The verses are listed with most effective or important Scriptures first.

1. *General Principles*

Romans 12:1–2	Matthew 10:37–39
1 Corinthians 3:16–17	1 Corinthians 6:12
1 Corinthians 8:1–12	1Corinthians 10:23–33
2 Corinthians 6:14–17	Galatians 5:16–17, 19–26
Galatians 2:20	Ephesians 5:5–14
Colossians 3:5–7	1 Peter 1:13–16
1 Peter 2:16	1 Peter 4:1–6

2. *Rebellion*
   Hebrews 13:17
   1 Samuel 15:22–23
   Ephesians 4:17–19

3. *Dishonesty*
   1 Peter 2:13–15
   Ephesians 4:17–25
   Proverbs 3:3

4. *Revenge*
   Romans 12:17–21
   1 Peter 3:9
   Hebrews 10:30

5. *Materialism and Greed*
   2 Corinthians 9:6–7;
   1 Timothy 6:6–11
   Hebrews 13:5
   Luke 12:16–34
   James 2:1–7

6. *Idolatry*
   Luke 10:38–42
   1 Corinthians 10:6–11
   Exodus 20:3–6

7. *Grumbling*
   Philippians 2:14
   James 4:1–7
   James 3:2–6

8. *Jealousy*
   James 3:14–15
   James 4:1–3
   2 Corinthians 10:12
   Galatians 5:26

9. *Anger*
   James 1:19–20
   Ephesians 4:26–32
   Matthew 5:22–24
   Proverbs 22:24–25

10. *Fear*
    Psalm 34:4–9
    Isaiah 26:3
    2 Timothy 1:7
    Isaiah 41:10
    John 14:27
    Joshua 1:9

11. *Slander and Gossip*
    Ephesians 4:29–32
    Proverbs 16:27–28
    Colossians 3:8
    James 4:11–12
    Galatians 5:13–15

12. *Depression*
    2 Samuel 22:29
    Psalm 34:15–19
    Jeremiah 17:16
    Isaiah 40:28–31

13. *Lust and Immorality*
    Ephesians 5:1–5
    1 Thessalonians 4:3–6
    Matthew 5:27–28
    Galatians 5:16–25
    1 Corinthians 6:18–20

14. *Impurity*
    Colossians 3:2
    2 Corinthians 10:5
    Philippians 4:8
    Romans 13:13–14

15. *Judging Wrongly*
    Matthew 7:1–5
    John 3:17

16. *Anxiety*
    Philippians 4:6–8
    1 Peter 5:6–7
    Matthew 6:25–34

17. *Pride*
    Proverbs 16:18–19
    1 Peter 4:5–7
    Proverbs 16:5

18. *Holding Grudges*
    Colossians 3:12–14
    Ephesians 4:26–27, 31–32
    Matthew 6:14–15

19. *Quarreling*
    1 Corinthians 3:3
    1 Corinthians 12:25
    James 4:1–3

20. *Selfish Ambition*
    Philippians 2:3–4
    1 Peter 5:6
    Proverbs 16:18–19

...THROUGH THE HOLY SPIRIT'S POWER

A tremendous resource for self-control that's available to every child who knows Jesus—and their parents—is the Holy Spirit. Here are the many ways the Holy Spirit can help us resist temptation and display self-control.

The Spirit guides	Isaiah 30:21; John 16:13
He teaches	John 14:26; 1 John 2:27
He changes attitudes	Galatians 5:22–23
He causes rejoicing	Ephesians 5:18–20
He gives peace	John 14:27; Galatians 5:22
He convicts of sin	John 16:8–11
He intercedes in prayer	Romans 8:26–27
He helps you have moral purity	Galatians 5:16–18
He witnesses in and through you	John 15:26–27; Acts 1:8
He strengthens you	Zechariah 4:6

He glorifies Jesus through you	John 16:14
He sanctifies us	2 Thessalonians 2:13
He gives us the mind of Christ	1 Corinthians 2:10–16
He gives power, love, and a sound mind	2 Timothy 1:7
He gives spiritual gifts	1 Corinthians 12
He gives life now and forever	Romans 8:10–11

BIBLICAL EXAMPLES TO USE IN TEACHING SELF-CONTROL

Many characters described in the Bible started well in their walk with God, only to fail badly because of a lack of self-control, which lead them into sin. Here are several:

King David — Known as a man after God's own heart, he did not guard his "downtime" and spiraled downward into an agonizing pit of adultery and murder (2 Samuel 11).

King Solomon — Tutored by godly Nathan, guided by his father David, and blessed by the hand of God, he developed the "I want what I want, when I want it" syndrome (Ecclesiastes 2:1–10). In the eloquent words of Chuck Swindoll, author and speaker, in his "Insight for Living" newsletter, "[Solomon] began to believe the lie that has captured many a top executive, or super salesman, or successful physician, or athletic prima donna, or film star, or TV celebrity, or gifted musician."

Samson — Although he distinguished himself as God's servant and Israel's deliverer from the Philistines as a Nazirite blessed with great physical strength, Samson revealed the secret of his strength by giving in to Delilah's enticements, and the Lord left him (Judges 13–16).

Esau — Though he was Isaac's first and favorite son, Esau sold his birthright to satisfy his appetite (Genesis 25).

Gehazi — At one time an obedient servant to godly Elisha, he was overwhelmed by greed and received what he did not seek—leprosy (2 Kings 5).

Eve	She was the mother of the human race, yet she gave up control when she chose to obey Satan rather than God when tempted by the lust of flesh and the lust of the eyes and the boastful pride of life (1 John 2: 16; see Genesis 3:6). Significantly, Eve and her husband, Adam, who sinned as well, witnessed the inauguration of the sacrificial system. Out of His great love for us, God ultimately gave up Jesus, who in turn chose to die on a cross as a sacrifice for all of us who would be born with a natural bent toward losing self-control (Genesis 3; Romans 3:24; 2 Corinthians 5:21).

On the other hand, God left us with plenty of examples of people practicing self-control:

Joseph	He controlled his anger when mistreated by his brothers and sold as a slave, and he controlled all temptation when enticed by his boss's wife. He resisted having anger toward God or others when unjustly sent to prison, and later his lack of anger allowed him to forgive and sustain life instead of retaliating against his brothers (Genesis 37–45).
Daniel	This exile in Babylon controlled his appetites, filled his downtime with prayer, used discretion and discernment rather than rebellion, and controlled his convictions by testifying about God at the risk of being killed (Daniel 1–2, 4–6).
Esther	Another exile living in Babylon, she had self-control to submit to the authority of her wise uncle; she controlled her aggression to do things in the wisest manner and as a result was chosen queen and saved her people (Esther).
Rahab	She controlled her tongue and was faithful to conceal God's messengers, and is included among the faithful (Joshua 2:1–16; Hebrews 11:31; James 2:25).

Stephen

Described as "a man full of faith and of the Holy Spirit" (Acts 6:5), he displayed self-control over his own desires so that he might serve the people of God and witness to the nonbelieving. He controlled his fear and preached with conviction. He was even able to control what anger or pride he may have had and asked the Lord to "not hold this sin against" the ones who were stoning him to death (Acts 7:60; Stephen's story is found in Acts 6–7).

Resource Four
Learning
Perseverance

The promises of the Scriptures can help your children to persevere during tough times. Here are several Bible verses you can direct them to during such days.

WHEN BURDENED BY SCHOOL, WORK, OR EXTRACURRICULAR ACTIVITIES

Psalm 138:8
Matthew 11:28–30
Romans 8:28, 35–39
Philippians 3:13–14
Colossians 3:23–24

James 1:1–12
Isaiah 40:28–31
Romans 13:1–5
2 Corinthians 12:9–10
Philippians 4:6–7, 13, 19

WHEN FEELING MISTREATED AND ALONE

1 Thessalonians 5:15–18
1 Peter 2:18–25
2 Corinthians 5:14
Hebrews 11
Colossians 3:2
Isaiah 41:10

Matthew 5:39–48
Proverbs 16:6–7
Isaiah 26:3
Psalm 50:15
Hebrews 13:5
John 14:18

WHEN SUFFERING OR FEELING DISCOURAGED OR DEPRESSED

Romans 8:18
Hebrews 12:1–4
Psalm 34:15–22
Romans 12:19
1 Peter 1:6–9
2 Corinthians 4:8–9

Psalm 30:5
Luke 6:21
Philippians 3:10–21
Psalm 42:11
John 14:1, 27
1 Peter 5:7

WHEN AFRAID

2 Timothy 1:7
Psalm 23
Psalm 4:8
Psalm 91
Psalm 46:1–3
1 John 4:18

Joshua 1:7–9
Psalm 27:1–14
Isaiah 41:10,13
Psalm 118:6
Romans 8:15
Romans 8:29, 31, 35–39